The Contented Baby Goes to School

Help your child to make a
calm and confident start

Gina Ford

Vermilion
LONDON

3 5 7 9 10 8 6 4 2

Published in 2014 by Vermilion, an imprint of Ebury Publishing

Ebury Publishing is a Random House Group company

The Random House Group Limited Reg. No. 954009
Addresses for companies within the Random House Group can be found at
www.randomhouse.co.uk

A CIP catalogue record for this book is available from the British Library

The Random House Group Limited supports The Forest Stewardship Council® (FSC®),
the leading international forest-certification organisation. Our books carrying the FSC label
are printed on FSC®-certified paper. FSC is the only forest-certification scheme supported
by the leading environmental organisations, including Greenpeace. Our paper procurement
policy can be found at www.randomhouse.co.uk/environment

Printed and bound by CPI Group (UK) Ltd, Croydon, CR0 4YY

ISBN 9780091947385

Copies are available at special rates for bulk orders. Contact the sales development team
on 020 7840 8487 for more information

To buy books by your favourite authors and register for offers, visit
www.randomhouse.co.uk

The information in this book has been compiled by way of general guidance in relation to
the specific subjects addressed, but is not a substitute and not to be relied on for medical,
healthcare, pharmaceutical or other professional advice on specific circumstances and in
specific locations. Please consult your GP before changing, stopping or starting any medical
treatment. So far as the author is aware the information given is correct and up to date as at
July 2014. Practice, laws and regulations all change, and the reader should obtain up to date
professional advice on any such issues. The author and publishers disclaim, as far as
the law allows, any liability arising directly or indirectly from the use, or misuse,
of the information contained in this book

The Contented
Baby Goes
to School

To all the parents who have supported me over the years.

Contents

Introduction

Your child's first day at nursery or school is a milestone for the entire family. This should be an exciting time for you and your child, but it can be a daunting experience, overshadowed by worries and concerns. It is only natural to feel some anxiety if this is the first time you will be leaving your child in someone else's care all day, but it can feel just as significant an event for parents who have been using a day nursery since their child was a baby – and your child may have fears of his own, too. There are quite likely to be some teething problems and it can take a while to get used to this major change in your lives, but feeling confident that you've made the right choices along the way, and knowing that you're as prepared as you can be, will make all the difference to both you and your child.

Your child may be entering a new phase of his life, but he still needs you now as much as – if not more than – before. My aim in this book is to ensure your 'Contented Baby' becomes a 'Contented Child' and that you as a parent stay contented, too! The same principles still apply: making sure your child's practical and emotional needs are met; being organised to make the day more enjoyable and stress-free; and, perhaps most importantly, giving your child a routine either side of the school day that will make him feel secure and cared for.

The right kind of nursery or pre-school education can be very beneficial to a child, helping to develop his social and educational skills. It offers a great start before more formal education begins, and enjoyable play-based learning can help establish your child's thirst for knowledge. At this stage, basic numeracy and literacy skills can be established in a low-key way through play, which aims to set children up for a good start once they begin formal education.

Of course, the educational skills children will learn are essential, but it is also the social skills needed for later success that begin to be established during this nursery/pre-school phase. Your child will take the first steps towards a degree of independence, and will start to build friendships with peers. Early-years education aims to prepare a child to be able to learn and develop: laying the ground rules for good behaviour; teaching children how to share with one another; setting boundaries and helping them understand the importance of following instructions. The principles of this stage of education include recognising the individuality of each child, helping them to foster relationships based on respect, providing the right environment to support their learning, and helping them to develop at the rate that is right for them. What is perhaps most important is that this kind of early learning can be a positive and enjoyable experience for young children, where they will have fun as they learn the skills they will need for the formal education that will follow.

Although you may be well aware that nursery, pre-school or reception is going to be good for your child, it's only natural to feel some concerns about this big step in your lives. It can be particularly difficult if it is your first, or only, child and you have never left him in the care of others before, but it's not just first-time parents who find this an emotional time – having been through this stage with older children doesn't necessarily make it less challenging this time round. The children themselves may have an unsettled period due to the big change in their daily routine, and this can be hard to deal with as a parent. Children do sometimes cry when they are left at nursery or pre-school, and it may feel heartbreaking to leave your child if he seems upset and doesn't want you to go. Understanding that this is usually a short-lived phase, and taking steps to ensure that you have done all you can to minimise any distress, will help you both to cope.

When you are leaving your toddler at nursery for the first time you will inevitably worry about how he will cope without one-to-one attention, and whether he has the necessary social skills to deal with such a large chunk of time away from you. Will your child remember to ask when he needs the potty? Will he feel lonely in a strange environment? How will he cope with all the other children? Will he remember to share without you there to remind him, and will he make friends? You may wonder how the nursery day will fit around your child's existing routines and whether any disruption to this will have an impact on how settled he is at home.

Starting in the reception class at 'big school' is a really exciting time, and marks the start of a whole new phase for both you and your child. Choosing the right school for your child and making sure that he is prepared can make the transition run more smoothly, but you may still have a host of practical concerns about how he will manage: Will he be frightened in the rough and tumble of the playground with so many older children? Will he be able to sit still and listen? Will he be able to do up his shoes or get changed into his PE kit without help? Will he remember to put on his coat at playtime? What happens if he doesn't like what he's given for lunch?

All parents experience some concerns when they leave their children for the first time, and this can be particularly difficult if you feel your child isn't quite ready for school. Summer-born children can be almost a year younger than some others in their class, and you may feel your child is not sufficiently mature to deal with the structure or length of the school day. Some children are more physically active than others, and if you have a lively child who needs to be outside and running about, the prospect of sitting down for longer periods of time may be challenging. Remember that teachers are used to handling this and that during the early years there is a fairly gentle transition to formal learning – it is recognised that play-based education can be far more effective for younger children.

I hope that this book will help calm any fears you have by offering practical solutions to ensure that you and your child are prepared for starting nursery or school. By including advice on how to minimise problems such as separation anxiety and regressive behaviour, giving tips on preparing your child for new routines and a different environment, and providing vital information to help you to equip your child with the skills he will need, I hope that this book will address any issues that may arise.

Starting school or nursery is a great adventure for you and your child. It is the start of a new stage in your lives and will be a big change for your whole family. I hope this book will ensure that the transition is a time of excitement and enjoyment rather than of worry and anxiety, and that your babies, toddlers and young children will remain as contented as ever throughout their early days at nursery, pre-school or school.

A note about types of care

- Day nurseries provide all-day childcare all year round from early age to school age. There are usually different rooms within the nursery, such as a baby room, toddler room and pre-school room. A child can join a day nursery at any time and most nurseries offer full-time or part-time hours.

- Private nursery schools are privately owned and usually take children from ages 2–5. Some follow the school term times, while others are open all year round.

- Nurseries attached to schools are known as maintained nurseries. They offer part-time, local education authority-funded care, following the school term, for children aged 3–5.

- Pre-schools take children from ages 3–5, offering part-time care, usually mornings or afternoons, and follow school term times and holidays.

- Reception class is the first year of primary school, for children aged 4–5.

1

Before Starting Nursery or Pre-school

When you begin to think about a nursery or pre-school for your toddler or older child, you will find a wide range of options available. You may want to start by spending some time considering what would work for you and for your child before making a decision. You may prefer a day nursery, which has the advantage of longer opening hours and can be the easiest option for working parents, or you may want to consider a playgroup, a state-run nursery school or a private nursery as an alternative option, depending on your family's needs and what you think would best suit your child.

As a child grows older, you will not only be thinking in terms of the most suitable form of childcare, but will also be focusing on the type of pre-school education on offer. You will want to consider what might be best for your child as an individual and what might benefit him most. Spending time at nursery or pre-school is generally useful for any child and many mothers who have opted to stay at home will still choose to send their child to nursery or a playgroup before he starts school in order to reap the benefits of pre-school education. Nurseries or pre-schools may only offer the option of a few relatively short sessions a week, but the regular pattern of spending some time in a pre-school setting can still have a positive effect. If your child has been with one main carer until this point, adjusting to being apart from that carer and taking the first steps towards independence can make the transition to school far easier. The social aspect of pre-school or nursery is equally important, as learning to get on with peers and just spending time in a group of other children can be a useful preparation for primary school, and children will be able to benefit from the range of different activities and learning opportunities on offer.

The Advantages of Nursery or Pre-school

Parents often feel quite anxious about sending a young child to a nursery or pre-school if he has always been looked after by one person, whether a parent or a carer. It is important to keep in mind that as a parent you may feel more anxious about this than your child does, and you should be careful not to project your own concerns on to your child. It can take a child a while to adjust to being in a completely different environment and to spending time with a group of others of the same age, but most children settle fairly quickly and there are some very clear advantages for children in attending a nursery or pre-school, even just for a few sessions a week.

- **Activities:** Nurseries and pre-schools offer a range of play-based learning opportunities for your child that you are unlikely to be able to offer at home. When you are looking after your child at home, your own daily activities and household chores will have to feature in your child's daily routine. At nursery, the entire session is focused on the children and their needs. Nurseries and pre-schools can often offer a huge variety of different activities to stimulate the children, such as painting, drawing, singing, music, outdoor play, imaginative play and dance. There will be a much wider range of toys and equipment than you can provide at home, and children can enjoy exploring these new play opportunities in the company of others of their own age.

When children first begin to play it is usually a solitary activity, where they are lost in their own world. As they grow older, they may begin to engage in parallel play, where they are playing next to rather than with another child but still keeping an eye on one another's activities. It is often around the time that they start nursery that they begin to play together more actively in co-operative play.

There is a wide range of different types of play that your child will be encouraged to enjoy at nursery, each of which will help develop different skills. At this age, children learn through play and a variety of play experiences will provide a rich and enjoyable learning experience. Creative play may involve using play-dough, paint or junk modelling. Physical activities will help develop gross and fine motor skills (actions that involve the movement of big and small muscles, respectively) and hand–eye co-ordination. Games with rules will help children to learn about taking turns and sharing. Language development is boosted by rhymes, songs, sounds and words, while imaginative play also helps to extend language and can develop your child's thinking and communication skills.

- **Curriculum:** There will be a planned curriculum to ensure that the activities on offer provide suitable learning opportunities for the children. Play-based learning allows the children to enjoy what they are doing without feeling any sense of pressure. It can help them learn some of the basic skills that they will need for the future in a relaxed environment and will help prepare them for the foundation stage at school. At this stage of early learning, the curriculum may include communication and language, physical development, literacy, numeracy, understanding of the world, expressive arts and design, and personal, social and emotional development. This may sound very formal, but for children at nursery and pre-school these are taught through play and in a low-key, enjoyable way.

- **Social skills:** It is often noted that young children seem to learn social skills more quickly in nursery, as they spend time playing and learning in a group. This can be one of the real benefits of early nursery education as it will help your child to understand the importance of sharing, taking turns and thinking about other people. Children of this age tend not to develop strong friendships, but they will start to play with one another and to have fun together. Spending time with other children will help your child appreciate how to get on with others of his own age more easily, and having well-developed social skills at a relatively early age can be a huge bonus.

- **Confidence:** Parents often find that their children grow in confidence once they start at nursery. Children develop a degree of independence at a nursery or pre-school as they have to learn to perform some simple tasks themselves, whereas at home it is all too easy to end up doing everything for them because it is quicker and easier. Even very shy children can begin to emerge from their shells if they are in a supportive environment. Of course, there may be an initial settling-in period when a child seems unhappy at being separated from a parent or carer and distressed when he is first left, but most get over this fairly quickly and mixing with a number of other children and adults during the day can help build a lasting confidence.

- **Language and communication skills:** At nursery or pre-school, staff will focus on children's communication skills, which helps to develop their language and the way they interact with others around them. Listening to stories regularly, joining in with group discussions on a specific topic, singing songs and rhymes and learning to pay attention when others are speaking are key elements of this early learning. Many children begin to learn about the letters of the alphabet at nursery or pre-school, helping them to see how written words are formed and the importance they have. They may start some work on sounds, talking about words which begin with specific letters of the alphabet. At nursery and pre-school children are not taught by sitting in rows at desks, but will absorb their learning through games and play. Children learn quickly at this age, especially if they are in a stimulating environment, and it is a time of rapid development for a child's language and communication skills.

- **Safety and security:** Nurseries and pre-schools offer a secure and safe environment. They are registered and inspected and have to meet certain requirements, such as having the right ratio of staff to children and ensuring that criminal records checks have been carried out on those working with the children. You can ask a nursery or pre-school about their inspection reports and ask to see these when you are making a decision about where to send your child. Parents sometimes feel more comfortable knowing that their child is being cared for by a group of people in a nursery setting than they would leaving them in the care of just one person.

- **Establishing a network:** It is not only children who start to make friends through nursery or pre-school. Parents will also have the opportunity to get to know other adults who have children of the same age. If you've been at home with your child, you have probably established some networks with other mothers already, but for working parents this can sometimes be quite difficult. Meeting other parents at nursery can give you the opportunity to make friends with people in your local area. This means your child can benefit from having playdates and you may find it beneficial to be able to share experiences with other parents, too.

- **Easing the transition to school:** One of the major benefits of attending nursery or pre-school is that it makes the transition to primary school much easier for children. Starting primary school is a major landmark in your child's life and the transition to school is likely to run more smoothly if your child is used to spending time with others of the same age in a pre-school setting. Having already gained a sense of independence and having started to develop social skills will give your child some clear advantages when it comes to starting school. What's more, you may find that some of the children your child meets at nursery or pre-school will be going on to the same primary school – knowing some familiar faces on the first day can also be a huge bonus.

What is the Best Age to Start?

Parents often worry about when would be the best time for a child to start nursery or pre-school, and with so many different options available it is not surprising that this can be a bit of a dilemma. Of course, in reality the best time to start nursery will vary from one child to another and will also be dependent on your own needs. If you need full-time childcare for a baby and come to the conclusion that nursery would be the best option, then your child may start in a day nursery at just three or four months old, although most mothers wait until at least six months old, and continue to be in full-time nursery care until he starts school. If you are a full-time parent, you may feel your child would enjoy joining a playgroup or you may choose to wait until he is old enough to join a state nursery at three, or you may feel he isn't ready to be in a group setting until shortly before he would be old enough to start in the reception class at primary school.

Generally, children do benefit from spending time with others of the same age and from the independence that a nursery or playgroup can give them before they start primary school. We know that it can make the transition to school easier if children have had some experience of being away from parents or carers and of looking after themselves in a group of others, but there is no one right answer about exactly how much nursery care is best or at what age a child should start. Don't forget that each child is an individual, and what suits one may not be best for another. When you're making these decisions, you need to be guided by what you think would be best for your child and for your family.

State nursery education is usually only provided for children who have reached the age of three, and parents sometimes assume that this means they will be guaranteed a place in a state nursery as soon as their child has celebrated his third birthday. In fact, funding is available from the start of the term after your child turns three, so this can involve a wait of some time – for example, a child born in May won't qualify for a place until September. Even then, depending on provision in your local area you may still have to wait a while to secure a place at a state nursery.

Playgroups may take children from two or two-and-a-half. Some children are perfectly happy to be left at playgroup or nursery at this age, and will settle in quickly and enjoy playing with their peers. Others may find it far more difficult and will need weeks of gradual settling in before they are happy to be left by themselves. Only you will know when your child seems ready. This is as much to do with the nature of the child as with age, and sometimes your child may surprise even you; a shy child may be quite happy to be left at nursery and to get on with things, while a more confident child can sometimes become anxious when he is taken out of his usual comfort zone.

Key Skills for Nursery and Pre-school

Some nurseries or pre-schools expect children to have a certain degree of independence before they start, and you should talk to the staff to make sure that you know what is expected. It is important to establish this when you are first considering a place at a pre-school or nursery in order to ensure that you have plenty of time to prepare your child, if necessary.

- **Potty-training:** If your child is starting nursery or pre-school at three years of age, he will be expected to be potty-trained before he joins – this can become a tricky issue if he isn't ready. Parents can end up getting into a race against time to potty-train their child in time for the starting date at nursery. It is essential to be realistic about this. If you have a child who is clearly not ready for potty-training, you can't force this through quickly so that he can start nursery when you'd like him to and expect things to go smoothly. Your child may sense if you are worrying about him having a toileting accident, which can be counter-productive and increase the likelihood of potty-training problems. Talk to the nursery if you are feeling pressured. It would be better to delay the start date a little if it is going to become a problem for you and your child.

When a child is ready for potty-training, it can be a surprisingly quick and painless business, but you can't bank on this and you need to allow time for your child to feel confident about using a potty. A nursery or pre-school will be a new setting, and sometimes even children who have been quite confident about using the potty at home can find it more difficult when they aren't in a familiar setting. Remember that it is perfectly normal for young children to have toileting accidents now and again, especially if they get very absorbed in an activity. The nursery staff will be used to dealing with this and should always react in a sympathetic and understanding manner. Most nurseries will ask you to leave some spare clothes there in case of toileting accidents, and many have their own supplies as well.

It is a good idea to try to get your child to use public toilets when you are out and about so that he isn't worried about this when he starts nursery or playgroup. Children are comfortable with familiarity and may try to put off going to the toilet if they feel worried about using different toilets.

- **Behaviour:** Nursery staff would not expect perfect behaviour from pre-school children, but it is important that your child is able to respect adults, respond to guidance and reprimands, and follow instructions. Children who have been set boundaries at home from an early age will find adapting to a nursery or pre-school environment far easier as they will understand the ground rules about what is expected of them. It goes without saying that young children won't always do everything that you ask of them, but if your child is able to follow instructions at home and has been taught to respect other adults, he is less likely to have behavioural problems at nursery or pre-school. It may be helpful to think about this in the time leading up to your child starting at nursery, and to make sure you encourage him to follow instructions.

A pre-school or nursery will have some rules about discipline, and when you are making a choice this can be an important topic to discuss. Ask about relevant behaviour and discipline policies, and about the methods of behaviour management that are employed if, for example, a child repeatedly disobeys instructions, has problems interacting kindly with other children or has a temper tantrum. You will want to be certain that you are happy with the way the nursery or pre-school deals with these issues. Trained staff will be experienced at dealing with children who are still finding their way with behaviour, but may use time-out sessions, cooling-down periods or even remove privileges when children are repeatedly disobedient.

Of course, it is not just discipline that is important but also praise for good behaviour and you may also find out how this is addressed. Some nurseries will give stickers and use star charts or rewards, and may give older children new privileges if they behave well, while others may focus on verbally responding positively to good behaviour.

- **Concentration:** Children are not expected to concentrate on one activity for long periods of time at nursery or pre-school, but your child should be capable of sitting still and listening to a story or joining in with a quiet activity. This can be difficult at first for children who are active and exuberant by nature and who enjoy racing about all the time. If you have a very active, fidgety child, it may take him a while to learn how to sit still in a group and listen. This is all part of the learning process at nursery or pre-school and is one of the reasons that nursery is such an excellent preparation for school, as your child will be used to following instructions and will have experience at sitting with others and listening. If you read regularly to your child from an early age and have encouraged him to enjoy some quiet activities, he is more likely to be able to sit still during story time or circle time at nursery.

- **Independence:** Before your child starts at nursery or pre-school, you can encourage him to develop some sense of independence by allowing him to make choices at home.

You will have done this without even realising it – for example, when you discuss which book to look at before bed, when you ask whether he wants an apple or a banana or when you let him choose which toys to get out. Take time to talk to the staff at the nursery or pre-school before your child starts and make sure you know what might be expected of him. You can then encourage him to do certain things or to make certain decisions by himself at home before he joins the nursery or pre-school. If you have opted to stay at home and look after your child, he may not be used to spending time with anyone else. If you feel this could be an issue, it may be helpful to go out for an evening now and then and get in a babysitter, or leave your child with a relative or friend for an hour or two. If your child feels confident about having a degree of independence, this will help him settle into nursery more easily.

- **Social skills:** Is your child able to share, to take turns and to play happily with other children? These are not quantifiable skills that nursery staff will want to tick off on a list, but it can be helpful if your child has spent time with children the same age and is aware of what may happen in group situations. Most children develop social skills gradually at nursery and it is perfectly normal for them to have problems with the concepts of sharing or taking turns at first. If your child has already experienced some group activities, this will help him adapt more quickly.

You can help your child prepare for this aspect of nursery or pre-school by ensuring that he has the opportunity to spend some time with others of the same age before he starts. Try to arrange some playdates or visits to see friends with children of his age, or take him to some mother and toddler or activity groups. If you have just one child this can be particularly important, but even children who have siblings will benefit from this – a much older brother or sister will not react in the same way as another child of the same age.

- **Practical skills:** It is a good idea to help your child learn some of the basic practical skills he may need in nursery – for example, taking his coat on and off and hanging it on a peg, pulling his clothes down to go to the toilet independently, wiping his own bottom and washing his hands, and putting on shoes to go outside. What is expected may differ from one nursery to another, so do talk to staff about their expectations, and make sure that your child is used to doing some of these things for himself. You can make it easier for him by thinking about what he wears to nursery – for example, shoes with Velcro fastenings and skirts or trousers with elasticated waists are a good idea. Tell the staff if your child struggles with some of these practical tasks so that they are aware of what he finds difficult. Most will be happy to offer support in the early days, but will expect a child to gradually learn to take responsibility for doing these things for himself.

Children may also be expected to carry out some basic chores at nursery, such as packing away toys. At home it is tempting to do such a task yourself because it is quicker, but if your child has learnt to do this when he's with you it will make the transition to nursery much more straight-forward. Your child will understand what is involved and be helpful.

Being able to feed himself is another important practical skill that is sometimes overlooked. Parents who find it quicker, easier and less messy to feed their toddlers themselves may not realise that their child has not learnt these skills properly. A child will need to be able to eat and drink independently at nursery or pre-school and, even though they may not always manage food perfectly at this age, they should be confident about using cutlery rather than their fingers and drinking from a beaker.

If you know your child is a fussy eater, you may be concerned about how he will cope with being given foods that he may not like at nursery. Some parents worry about this a lot, but it is often the case that children will eat all kinds of things at nursery that they wouldn't touch and claim not to like at home!

There are some tips that may help fussy eaters at nursery:

- Do make nursery staff aware of your child's likes and dislikes, but be realistic about how much they can pander to this. It is not possible for staff to prepare completely different meals for a child who is very fussy, but nurseries are used to catering for small children's tastes and your child will probably find some foods he likes on the menu even if it isn't all to his taste.

- Explain to your child that he may find food on his plate at nursery that he wouldn't have chosen, but that it is all right to leave things if he doesn't feel he can eat them.

- Give your child a good breakfast at home before he goes to nursery so that you can ensure he is well set up for the day.

- Make sure he has a drink before nursery, too. Children will usually be given drinks at regular intervals throughout the day, but it's still a good idea to make sure he has something before you set off in the morning.

- Some nurseries will keep a diary of what your child has eaten so that you know exactly how much he has consumed during the day, but others may not have the time or resources for this. If you feel that your child may not be eating properly at nursery, discuss this with the staff.

- Have a healthy snack and a drink to hand when you pick your child up as he is bound to be hungry. It is quite normal for children to feel ravenous after nursery or pre-school and this doesn't necessarily indicate that your child hasn't eaten enough during the day, but more that he has been busy rushing about and burning up lots of energy!

● **Educational skills:** Some parents are very keen for children to start formal education at an early age, and start teaching numbers and letters as soon as they can in the belief that this will mean their child is academically ahead of his peers in the future. In fact, there is some evidence that very early formal learning isn't always a good idea, and in many countries children don't start any formal education until they are at least six years of age. If your child is interested and enjoys learning then that's fine, but it isn't a good idea to try to force a young child to sit and learn if he clearly doesn't want to do this. There is no need for children to have any particular skills with numbers or letters before they join a nursery or playgroup – the only one that can be really useful is the ability to recognise their own name. However, even this is far from essential. Nursery or pre-school is about learning through play because this is how children learn best at this age, and they will all learn at different speeds.

Is my child ready for nursery or pre-school?

1. Is he potty-trained? Many pre-schools and nurseries will only take children who are potty-trained.

2. Is he used to spending some time apart from you?

3. How does he react when he is left with other people, such as babysitters?

4. Does he like being with other children?

5. Does he seem confident when he's in a group of others of his age?

6. Is he able to sit and listen when you read a story?

7.   Will the nursery routine disrupt his regular sleep times?

8.   Do you feel he is ready to broaden his horizons at nursery or pre-school?

9.   Do you feel ready for him to go to nursery or pre-school?

Different Types of Nursery and Pre-school

There are many different types of nursery or pre-school and the wide range of choice in some areas can be confusing at first. For most parents, the initial choice is driven by their own needs. If you want an extended day's childcare, you could use a day nursery or wrap around care with a childminder or nanny. You may also consider a playgroup which he will attend for just a few hours once or twice a week. Before you start looking at nurseries and pre-schools, it is advisable to sit down and think about what you want to ensure that you are looking at the right places to meet your requirements. Write a list of what you will need from a nursery and also of any aspects of nursery care that you feel would particularly benefit your child and use this as a starting point when you are making your decision.

Day nurseries

The day nursery caters for children from a very early age, sometimes taking children who are just three or four months old. A day nursery offers full-time care, usually right through the working day from around 8am to 6pm. Day nurseries are open during school holidays, and many are only shut for a few days each year on Bank Holidays and Christmas, although others may close for longer periods at certain times of year. A day nursery is a good option for working parents who are looking for childcare. Most will be able to offer different days and sometimes hours, too, so a child may only attend for one or two days a week and may only be there for half-days. The children attending a day nursery are usually divided into groups depending on their age, and the different age groups will often be in different rooms in the building. Many day nurseries cater for children until they are ready to start school, so this can provide a seamless form of childcare and nursery provision right through to primary school.

State nursery schools

Some state-run nurseries are attached to primary schools and feed into them, while others stand alone, only catering for pre-school children. If you are working full-time and want to send your child to a state nursery school, you will need additional childcare as state nurseries usually take children for a few hours at a time, often offering morning or afternoon sessions. Some state nursery schools do have a few full-time school-hours days available for children who are close to reception age, but working parents will usually have to have alternative childcare for the rest of their working day.

Children are entitled to a state nursery place from the beginning of the school term after their third birthday. In some areas there is pressure on nursery places and you may have to wait until a place becomes available. Some nurseries operate waiting lists. You can contact nurseries direct to find out what the current situation is with places. There is no charge for state nurseries once your child is the right age to qualify for state nursery education, but at the time of writing, the funding only covers 15 hours a week so you will have to pay for any additional hours yourself if the nursery can offer them. Most nurseries will only be open during school term times, so working parents will need childcare to cover the holidays. Classes are taught by qualified teachers and can be fairly large.

There are some state-run nursery schools that operate as Children's Centres or Early Years Education Centres. Some of these may take much younger children from just a few months old and offer full-time childcare, but this kind of provision is relatively rare.

Workplace nurseries

Some large companies may provide workplace nurseries or crèches for their employees, but there has been a decline in the numbers of workplace nurseries in recent years. A workplace crèche or nursery can be an ideal solution where it is available, as you will be able to be close to your child all day and you won't have to travel to take them to nursery before you start your own journey to work. If you have a long commute, however, you may not like the idea of your child having to do this journey with you each day. There are often fewer places available in workplace nurseries than there are parents who would like to take them up, so there can be waiting lists. Of course, one disadvantage of this type of childcare is that you will need to look for an alternative if you move jobs.

Private nursery schools

Not all fee-paying nurseries are day nurseries that take children from an early age. Some only take children from two or three years of age until they start school. They may offer a particular type of educational approach, for example Montessori nurseries or Steiner kindergartens (see below). Some fee-paying private nurseries are open for most of the year, but others will close during school holidays. Fee-paying nurseries may be open for a normal school day until about 3pm, or may provide childcare throughout the full working day.

Montessori nursery

Many nurseries call themselves Montessori, but the extent to which they follow the Montessori ethos may vary considerably. Montessori education is based on the theories of an Italian doctor, Maria Montessori, who set up her first school in Rome more than a hundred years ago. She believed that all children are motivated to learn and that they have absorbent minds. She felt that children could exceed expectations if they were presented with the right activities at the right time, and she was firmly against any form of testing or grading as she believed this was damaging to children's growth.

A true Montessori nursery will encourage children to focus on one activity at a time. They will be able to choose their own activities and the method involves learning through the senses. They spend a lot of time working alone, observed by their teachers. A Montessori nursery should have proper Montessori equipment such as wooden cylinders graded by size, wooden rods and tablets in different colours, sandpaper letters, wooden bricks and frames to practise lacing or tying. Everything is child-sized in a Montessori nursery and the children are encouraged to carry out real-life practical tasks, such as cleaning and washing, for themselves. The classroom is ordered and organised, but children are also encouraged to spend time outdoors, too, where again they get involved in real-life activities such as gardening.

If you are interested in a Montessori education for your child, it is worth doing some research to find out more about the theories behind it so that you can assess how closely any Montessori nursery you are considering follows the Montessori theory. In a true Montessori school, the teachers will be Montessori-qualified and this is important because they will have been trained to 'direct' the children to learning opportunities rather than actually 'teach'. The children are always taught in mixed age groups in Montessori nurseries, there should be a range of materials available and the children should be allowed to choose what they want to do, working individually for most of the time.

Steiner kindergarten

A nursery that follows the educational theories of Rudolf Steiner is usually known as a Steiner or Waldorf kindergarten. Rudolf Steiner was an Austrian philosopher who set up his first school in 1919 to cater for the children of the employees at the Waldorf-Astoria cigarette company in Germany. Rudolf Steiner's educational beliefs centre on the idea that children's creative, spiritual and moral needs are just as important as their intellectual needs.

You won't find plastic toys in a Steiner kindergarten, and there are unlikely to be any computers or even many books. The surroundings are thought to be very important and so a Steiner kindergarten will aim to offer a calm, natural and beautiful environment. The idea is to develop children's own imaginations so they will usually play with simple wooden toys or natural materials. Time spent outdoors is an important part of the daily routine to encourage children to experience nature and the seasons. There are often craft activities such as baking, weaving, sewing and painting. Rather than reading a book to the whole group of children in circle time, there will be a story told by the teacher and songs, poems and movement. Children may also join in with a dance form known as eurythmy, a type of performance art that is used to encourage self-expression. If you are considering a Steiner kindergarten for your child, you may be asked not to expose him to television or computers as it is thought these can be harmful to children's early development.

Private nursery that leads into an independent school

Some independent schools have their own nurseries, which then lead into pre-prep or preparatory departments. This can be an advantage for parents who have decided that they will want an independent education for their child. If you know you will want to opt for a particular prep school, then sending your child to the nursery at the same school can make the transition much easier – and may also help you to secure a place at the pre-prep or preparatory school. The downside of these nurseries is that they are usually term time only, even if they can sometimes offer a longer day to help working parents, and you may want to bear in mind the fact that independent schools often have fairly lengthy school holidays. Even the nursery departments of these schools may be selective, and may only offer places to children after an interview or some form of testing.

Pre-school playgroup

A pre-school playgroup may just run for a few hours a day and is an addition to existing childcare for working parents rather than an alternative. Some playgroups are run from church halls or community centres as most don't have their own permanent premises. A playgroup is often a far cheaper option than a nursery, and may take children from the age of two or three for short sessions of group play. Playgroups will usually have a qualified or experienced supervisor, but may sometimes be run with unqualified assistance or even parent volunteers. You may also come across some playgroups where parents are expected to stay with their children throughout the session, and these can be a good stepping stone towards nursery or pre-school.

Choosing the Right Nursery to Meet Your Family's Needs

It is important that the nursery or pre-school you select is right for your family. It will need to meet your childcare needs and feel like the best environment for your child. It is important to start thinking about this early, and give yourself at least a few months to find the right place for you and your family.

The first step is to think about what you need:

- How many hours a day would you like your child to attend the nursery?

- Do you need a nursery that provides year-round childcare, or are you happy to choose somewhere that is only open during school term time?

- When would you like your child to start?

- Will you want him to stay at the nursery until he is ready for primary school?

Your local council or education authority should be able to direct you to a list of nurseries in the area, and you may want to ring around a few and talk to them before going on to arrange visits to any suitable contenders. There are some key areas you may want to ask about at this stage; for example, the opening hours, the age of children the nursery provides for and the number of children and staff at the nursery. You may want to know about the outside space at the nursery or the curriculum. You will quickly start to get a feel for what you like and don't like. Do also check Ofsted inspection reports (see www.ofsted. gov.uk), which the nursery should be able to direct you to.

Make sure you visit any nursery you are considering. Initially, you may want to visit without your child so that you can spend time focusing on talking to the staff and establishing whether the nursery is suitable for your needs. Do go back again and take your child and see how he reacts to the nursery environment and how the staff react to him. Try to visit at a different time of day when you go back for the second time.

There are a number of key points you may want to make sure you have thought about:

- What are the opening hours? If you are working, you will want to work out how the opening and closing times will fit around your working day and whether you will need to arrange additional wrap-around childcare.

- How long are the holidays and when are they? While some day nurseries only shut on public holidays, most other nurseries will close for at least a week at Christmas and Easter, during half-term weeks and for a longer period over the summer. There may be clubs for children during the holidays, but this is something you will want to check.

- How will you get your child to and from the nursery? Think about the length of the journey and how you will deal with this on a daily basis.

- What qualifications do the staff have? In a state nursery, you can expect staff to have the relevant qualifications but it is always worth checking in other settings and find out how many staff have first-aid qualifications.

- Have all the staff undergone criminal record checks?

- If possible, find out what the staff turnover is like. You could ask other local mums who use the nursery about this. If the turnover is very high, it can be disruptive and could also indicate that staff are not entirely happy at the nursery.

- What is the ratio of staff to children? There are minimum requirements for this that are set depending on the age of the children, but some nurseries have fewer children for each member of staff.

- How big a group of children would your child be in? The size of classes can vary considerably in nurseries and playgroups, and this is something you will want to consider.

- Will your child have a key worker? Having a good key worker will make things far easier for your child as it can help him to settle in and feel confident, and is also good for you as it means that you have an initial point of contact for any worries, concerns and progress updates.

- How does the nursery communicate with parents? Nurseries often send messages and news home to parents by email or text. It is also a good idea to check how you will be expected to communicate with staff at the nursery.

- If you are going to have to pay, what are the fees and how are they payable? It is often possible to pay monthly by direct debit rather than forking out for a whole term in advance, which can make it easier to manage your finances.

- Does the nursery have any spaces for the time you are looking for and does it operate a waiting list? This is crucial as there is no point in spending hours pondering over a choice of nurseries only to discover that the one you decide on will not have any spaces available. For a state nursery, places tend to be allocated on catchment area, unless you have an older child who is already at the school. Be aware that you may not be given a place at the state nursery of your choice if it is some way from your home.

- How many children are there in total at the nursery? They can range from tiny nurseries with just a dozen children or so to big early years centres that may have more than a hundred children in a number of separate classes and feel more like a primary school.

- Do they provide meals for the children? School meals have been the subject of much discussion in recent years, and they do vary in quality. Ask what food is provided and when. Are meals cooked on site? Look at the menus to ensure you are happy with what the children are fed, and to check that there is a good variety of foods. If your child has any allergies or specific dietary requirements, ask how the nursery will deal with this. Some nurseries aim to provide seasonal, locally produced food and others only use free-range eggs and meat or even organic food. Ask about this if it is something that is important to you.

- Is there any outside space and how much time do the children spend there? For young children, spending time outside is very important so do ask to see the outside space, preferably at a time when the children are using it. Look at the facilities that are available, such as climbing frames and outdoor toys.

- Do the premises look clean? An organised, clean space is always more welcoming for children and parents. One place parents don't often get shown on open days is the toilets, but since your child will be using them it is quite valid to ask to take a look!

- Are the premises safe? Are gates and doors kept securely locked? Is the outside space fenced in?

- Are there plenty of toys and equipment to stimulate the children? You want your child to be in a stimulating environment so do look at the play activities provided.

- Ask about the structure of the day. Is there a regular story time and singing or music?

- How is the curriculum planned and how is progress monitored? How are achievements recorded? How will you be kept informed about your child's progress?

- Are activities structured to encourage the children's development?

- Are there opportunities for extra-curricular lessons, such as languages?

- Is there plenty of space for the children? Does the nursery feel comfortable to you?

- What are the policies for dealing with behaviour? You may want to ask not only how bad behaviour is addressed, but also whether there is a reward system in place for good behaviour.

- Do the children look happy? Of course, the key to a good nursery is happy children and you should take time during a visit to watch the children and see whether they seem to be enjoying themselves and how they interact with the staff.

- Have you looked at the inspection reports for the nursery? These can be found online and the nursery staff themselves should be happy to point you in the right direction. Inspection reports can highlight any particular strengths and weaknesses and this may help your decision-making.

- What is the local reputation of the nursery and what do other parents say about it? Mums' networks can often give interesting insights into the different nursery options in your area. Parents with experience of particular nurseries may be able to give tips that you wouldn't get from a visit. Other people's views can be helpful, but it is important that you make your own assessment, too. Don't automatically assume that what suits another family will be right for you, and don't dismiss a nursery just because another parent hasn't liked it without taking a look yourself.

- What is the nursery's settling-in policy? Nurseries are used to settling new children, and may have their own preferred methods of ensuring they feel happy about being left at nursery. Some will suggest that you take your child into nursery for brief periods before your official start date so that the change is easier, or that you stay for a while on your child's first few days, but make sure you have asked about this and that you are happy with what the nursery recommends.

- What is the atmosphere like? I believe your gut instinct can be your most important indicator when choosing a nursery. However marvellous a place may look and however many excellent policies the staff may seem to have in place, if something doesn't feel quite right to you, then don't ignore your instincts. Go to look at another nursery, or a few more, and see how they compare before making a decision. The atmosphere of a nursery is really important, and you aren't going to feel happy leaving your child if you aren't confident about the nursery or have some nagging doubts.

The last point about atmosphere may seem the least significant, but it is actually one of the most important factors to take into consideration when choosing a nursery. You should never underestimate the importance of your gut instincts when you're looking around nurseries for your child. If somewhere doesn't feel right to you, then it is unlikely to be right for your child either. If your child is old enough to express an opinion, do listen to him, too.

You will probably find that if you visit a few nurseries, it starts to become clearer that there are some things you like and others that you don't. You may want to draw up a shortlist before making a final decision, which may be influenced by which nursery has places available at the right time.

How to Prepare Your Child Emotionally

It is important to do all that you can to ensure that your child feels happy at the prospect of starting nursery, rather than anxious or concerned. There are some simple steps you can take to try to help the early days run as smoothly as possible. Much of it is to do with communicating clearly with your child about what is going to happen and when. Of course, this can be difficult with a younger child who may not entirely understand everything that you might want to tell him, but you can adjust your explanation to his understanding.

- Talk to your child about the nursery beforehand in a positive tone. Explain all the exciting things that he will be able to do there and make sure it sounds as if it will be fun.

- Explain clearly to your child when he will be starting nursery, how long he will be spending there, what he will do and who will be collecting him. It will be far easier for a child to settle if he knows who will be collecting him and when.

- Take your child to visit the nursery again before he is due to start so that he is familiar with the environment and give him the opportunity to see some of the activities that he will be able to take part in.

- There are lots of children's books about starting nursery (see page 201 for some recommendations) and you may want to track down some of these and look at them together as this can be very reassuring.

- If your child seems anxious, do encourage him to talk about any worries or fears he may have. Sometimes children can get very worried about small things and anxieties can easily build up if they are not addressed.

- Try to build up the amount of time your child spends away from home and with other people. You could arrange to go out for an hour or two leaving your child with a relative, friend or babysitter and gradually increase the amount of time you spend away in the weeks leading up to nursery.

- Tell your child lots of positive stories about other children's experiences of nursery – or even your own if you can remember them!

- If there are going to be any changes in your child's routine once he starts nursery, such as mealtimes and bedtime, try to introduce them in advance so that he is prepared for this and the transition is easier.

- If at all possible, try to introduce your child to other children who will be going to the nursery or who have already started there. Seeing a familiar face on the first day can make all the difference.

- Talk to the nursery about their preferred settling-in procedures and discuss this with your child so that he is clear about what will happen. He may find it much easier to cope with the first day if he knows you are going to stay for the first hour and then just leave him briefly, or that you will be there for part of the time for the first few weeks.

Parents often feel far more anxious than their children about the thought of leaving them at nursery or pre-school. If you want your child to enjoy the experience, you must try not to transmit your fears. Don't discuss any concerns you may have with your partner or other people when your child is there, and make sure you always talk about nursery in a positive, upbeat manner – but don't overdo it as children are perceptive and will pick up on this.

One key area to focus on when you are thinking about how to prepare your child for nursery is his confidence. Young children can easily feel at sea in an unfamiliar environment and when faced with new tasks and activities. Working to boost your child's self-esteem at this time can be beneficial, and there are some simple steps you can take to try to help your child to tackle the new challenges of nursery or pre-school with confidence.

- A child who is about to start nursery or pre-school can feel more vulnerable. Don't forget to remind him regularly that you love him and to show plenty of affection through hugs and kisses.

- Focus on praising your child's good behaviour rather than reprimanding him when he slips up.

- If you are worried that practical daily tasks may prove difficult for him, spend some time beforehand doing these together. Praise effort rather than achievement, and make it clear that it is having a go at things that matters rather than the perfect execution of any tasks.

- Arrange some playdates for your child in the lead-up to him starting nursery so that he gets used to spending time with other children.

- Playing some simple board games together can help your child to understand the importance of taking turns, which is going to be an important skill at nursery. Devoting time to this will not only help develop this skill, but is also an opportunity to spend some quality time with your child.

- Spending a little extra time together when he goes to bed, or at another quiet time during the day, will help to ensure your child feels loved and wanted and will give him a space to express any fears he may have.

Remember that all children are different, and don't expect your child to respond to starting nursery in exactly the same way that your friend's children or older siblings or relations have. Parents often worry that it is their fault if their child doesn't want to be left at nursery or finds it hard to adjust, but some of this is down to temperament.

If you have always followed my Contented Baby routines and have your child in a daily routine that works well, you may be worried about the disruption to the regular pattern of your child's days if he is going to be at nursery or pre-school full-time. In fact, nurseries have their own daily routines and meals and snacks will always be at the same time, so you may find that there is less disruption than you might expect. The one difficulty that can occur is when a child is used to having a nap during the day and this is no longer possible at the usual time, but this is something you will need to take into consideration when you are choosing a nursery.

Settling in can be more tricky if you have a child who is inclined to be difficult or resistant to change. If you know that your child is sometimes aggressive or tends to be hyperactive, if he really can't concentrate or sit still at all, or if he has frequent temper tantrums, you may worry about how he will cope at nursery. There are some issues you may wish to consider:

- Remember that it is very common for children to go through phases of difficult or challenging behaviour, and this is often something that they grow out of with boundaries, guidance and support.

- Sometimes children who can be quite challenging at home behave very differently at nursery where they are in a less familiar setting, and where the expectation is that they will behave well.

- Boundaries are essential and sometimes children who are difficult need nothing more than some structure and boundaries. Make sure that you are setting clear boundaries for your child at home that are not at odds with what is expected at nursery. If your child is used to you giving in to his demands, he is bound to find it more difficult to adapt to nursery where boundaries are set and followed.

- If you are worried about a child who is particularly difficult, don't be embarrassed to discuss this with staff beforehand. It is far better that they are forewarned. Experienced nursery staff will have seen all kinds of behaviour over the years, and will have strategies in place to deal with potential problems.

- Make yourself aware of the nursery policies on discipline and behaviour, and if they regularly use time-out or reflection sessions, explain this to your child beforehand so that he knows what will happen if he doesn't behave.

How to Prepare Yourself

Parents spend a lot of time thinking about finding the right nursery for their children, and worry about how they will settle in and whether they will like it, but rarely focus on how they are feeling about this change. It can be particularly difficult as a parent if your child is not initially keen on going to nursery and takes a while to settle in. It is very distressing to leave a young child upset or in tears when you are not going to see him for a few hours, or even for the rest of the day. It is worth remembering that most children, even if they seem upset at the moment of parting, will not spend the whole day feeling sad but will get on and enjoy the activities set up for them. There are some tips that may help you as a new nursery or pre-school parent:

- Remember that feeling some degree of separation anxiety is just as normal for you as it is for your child. It shows the bond between you and it would be odd if you didn't feel some worries and concerns about leaving him at nursery or pre-school for the first time. For reassurance, phone the nursery an hour or so after you've left your child to find out if he has settled. Most nurseries will actively encourage you to do this.

● Don't forget that you have spent some time looking at different nurseries or pre-schools. Be confident that you have chosen an environment where you think your child will be happy and that you will be leaving him there in the hands of professional staff who are used to caring for young children.

● It is very important not to let your child be aware of any worries that you have about nursery. Keep positive for him and you will find that it helps you to feel more positive yourself as you remind him of all that he has to look forward to.

● Starting nursery or pre-school is an important first step towards independence, and it is vital that you begin to learn to let go as a parent and to let your child have his first taste of life apart from you. Seeing how this helps him to grow and flourish will make you feel better about it yourself.

If you have made the effort to ensure that the nursery or pre-school you have chosen is suitable for you and for your child, and have spent some time preparing the ground with your child in advance, the chance of things going wrong in the early days will be greatly reduced. Children like familiarity and routine, and it is the sudden change in their daily pattern that can cause difficulties when they first start at nursery or pre-school. If you have managed to gradually introduce some of the changes that will be necessary and have prepared your child emotionally and equipped him with all the necessary practical skills, this will make things far easier. Paving the way by talking about nursery and discussing what lies ahead in a positive manner will ensure your child has the right attitude and this will make things far easier not only for your child, but also for you, too. Preparation really is the key to ensuring that you can both enjoy what should be an exciting new step forwards in your lives.

Case History: Ezra – Preparing for Nursery

Ezra is three and I knew I didn't want him to have a formal start to his education at such a young age. When I was looking for a nursery for my oldest child (Ezra is the youngest of four), I read up on everything and looked at all the Ofsted reports. I chose a nursery that could offer organic meals and lots of educational benefits, but I soon realised these benefits aren't so essential when you're looking at nurseries because most of what the children do is playing anyway. I had to drive to the nursery with my oldest daughter every day, and then drive her back at lunchtime and sometimes she would fall asleep in the car, which would upset her routine for the rest of the day. I think if you can, it's good to choose a nursery that doesn't involve a long car journey home and one that's in your own community.

I chose Ezra's nursery because it was small, with only about 15 children, and very homely. The staff know all the children, and it's very informal but they seemed to be able to teach the children without them even knowing it.

The nursery didn't have any particular requirements about what the children had to be able to do before they started, except for being potty-trained. Ezra has always been used to being with other children anyway because he's the youngest of four and the older ones always have friends round, so that wasn't a concern.

From an early age, I was never worried about letting other people hold Ezra and I think that made him more relaxed from the start. I did make sure he was used to being left before he started nursery, though. I used to take him to the crèche when I went to the gym to do an exercise class. They gave you up to three free settling-in sessions where you could stay with your child, and after that I would leave him there. He was happy for the most part but they did have to come and get me sometimes – I think it helped him to get used to being left. From when he was very little I used to take him to playgroups where I had to stay with him, and that helped him get used to being with others of his own age.

We've always read him a story in bed, and I think reading to children is important. It does help to prepare them. He's quite good at concentrating, although he's not like his older sisters who by his age would be sitting down and trying to write – they were just very keen, but he needs to run about more. He can sit down and listen, but it does have to be something he finds interesting.

We do have a routine, which I think has made it easier for him to settle. He does swimming and a music class with a friend, and his friend's mum and I take it in turns to take them to the classes. It's a nice way for them both to have some independence in a very safe way.

I also used to take him to a drop-in crèche at our local school twice a week for a couple of hours from when he was about 18 months old. That was very helpful in preparing him for nursery, because he was used to being in that kind of environment. At his nursery they are very relaxed about the settling-in stage anyway, and they are quite happy for parents to come in and stay for as long as they like. He settled very quickly, though, and I think the preparation we'd done beforehand helped with that. I do think leaving them for the first time is often worse for the parents than for the child.

2

The First Days and Weeks at Nursery or Pre-school

Making sure things run smoothly in the first few days and weeks at nursery is important – it can help to give your child a positive attitude towards education and shape the way he feels about it in the future. Getting it right at this stage can also give him a huge confidence boost as he will see that gaining some independence is fun and exciting rather than worrying or frightening. There will be hiccups along the way and it may take time for your child to settle and for you both to feel comfortable, so try not to get stressed about it. If you can adopt a relaxed attitude during these early days, or at least appear to be adopting a relaxed attitude, it can make all the difference.

Settling In

Most nurseries and pre-schools will encourage you to take your child for some trial settling-in sessions before he joins. Your child will have strong attachments to you and anyone else who has been looking after him, and it will take him time to adjust to being cared for by new adults in a nursery setting. If you just dropped him off on the first day and went to work for the day leaving your child, he would probably feel frightened and worried. If he's had some settling-in time, so that he has come to realise that the nursery is a safe environment and he knows who he can turn to if he has any worries, this will enable him to relax and enjoy nursery rather than feeling fearful and unhappy.

If your child has been in some other form of group care, such as a crèche or day nursery, in the past, it may be easier for him to settle if this has been a positive experience. The settling-in process is a balance between accepting the gradual withdrawal from you or his nanny or childminder, and the increasing familiarisation with the nursery. It can take time to get this right, and that is why the settling-in process is so important.

Nurseries tend to have established protocols for the settling-in period and these will differ from one place to another. The nursery staff will have established their system based on what they have found works and also what they have found minimises disruption for the other children. Generally, it is advisable to follow their suggestions and stick to the settling-in pattern they advise. However, if you are really worried that their proposed settling-in method won't suit your child or that he may take longer to settle in than the nursery is suggesting, make time to go and talk to staff about this. It may be that they are right and your child will settle in the way that they are anticipating, but remember that you know your child and if you are really concerned that their protocol for the settling-in period won't suit him, then don't be afraid to say so.

Once you have accepted a place at the nursery and set a starting date, the first part of the settling-in process is usually another visit to the nursery for you and your child. The aim of this will be to help familiarise your child with the new environment, the staff and all the other children. It also gives you the opportunity to spend a little more time at the nursery yourself, and to talk to staff, raising any questions or concerns that may have arisen since you accepted the place. At this stage, you will usually meet your child's key worker. Most nurseries and some playgroups run a key worker scheme, where each child is allocated to a particular member of staff, who becomes a main point of contact for the family. The key worker plays a pivotal role in the settling-in process, as he or she will be able to start forming a bond with your child. During the weeks and months ahead, the key worker will be responsible for monitoring your child's progress and development, and for checking that his needs are being met during his time at nursery.

Some nurseries or pre-schools may suggest what appears to be a very drawn-out settling-in period, and busy parents may be left wondering why they need to spend quite so many days visiting the nursery before their child builds up to spending a full day there. It may be that your child will settle quickly and a prolonged transitional period won't be necessary, but taking things gradually ensures that the change can be taken gently and that it always feels safe for your child. If your child does feel that things are going too quickly and becomes anxious or insecure about nursery, it can be hard to reverse this and rebuild his confidence. The more time your child spends in the nursery before he actually starts properly, the easier it will be for him to settle. He will be familiar with the daily routine of the nursery and will have had time to develop a positive relationship with the other children and the staff, in particular his key worker. If you have spent some time visiting the nursery, initially staying with your child and then leaving him for short periods of time, this can make the separation process far easier.

Some nurseries may like you to visit once a week over a longer period before starting, while others will prefer to fit the settling-in period into the week or two weeks before your child starts. Generally on the first visit you will stay with your child at the nursery for an hour or two. He will be encouraged to join in with all the activities and you can take a back seat role, allowing his key worker and other staff to spend time talking to him and encouraging him to get involved. On the second visit, you may leave your child briefly – perhaps staying in the building – and then by the third visit you may be able to leave him for an hour or two, or even half a day. There may be as many as four or five or more visits like this, where you leave your child for a little longer each time. There is no right or wrong way to do this and it is important to stress that different nurseries will do this in different ways for all kinds of reasons, and will have established a system that works for them. For some children, the settling-in period will be more than enough for them to be ready and looking forward to starting nursery properly, but others will be more reticent and may take far longer to feel happy about being left. Every child is different and so the settling-in period will need to be adjusted accordingly and you will need to discuss your child's progress with the nursery or pre-school as you go and work out the best way to proceed.

If your child is going to be spending a full day at nursery, it is a good idea to visit at different times of day during the settling-in period so that he is familiar with the pattern of the day for the whole time he will be there. Try to make sure that he uses the toilet at some point during the settling-in period, too, as it is important that he knows where to go and what the nursery facilities are like. He also needs to feel confident about who to turn to if he is worried or unhappy about something. This is most likely to be his key worker, and you may want to talk to him about talking to him or her.

The settling-in process can take some time and it is important to be patient at this stage as you will need to be led by your child's pace. Remember that this will give your child his first taste of independence and that the more positive an experience you can make this, the better it will be for his future development. Of course, it's not just about his happiness but also yours. You will be able to feel far more positive about leaving your child at nursery if you know he is happy and confident about being there.

The duration of the settling-in period will of course also be affected by the amount of time your child is going to be spending at nursery. If your child is going to be spending a full day at nursery five days a week, it may take a little more time to adjust than if he is going to be spending a few hours at a playgroup a couple of times a week. Some nurseries don't advocate such a prolonged settling-in period and may have established their own protocols for a shorter pattern that they have found to be successful. It is also not always possible to have a longer period if you have had to find a last-minute place for your child for some reason.

Separation Anxiety

Separation anxiety is all about your child's attachment to those who care for him and make him feel safe and secure. Babies often begin to experience separation anxiety from the age of 6–8 months, and can last for some time. Once your child has started to understand who you are and that you care for him, it is inevitable that he will worry when you are not there as he doesn't yet understand that you will come back. With time, and with repeated short separations, your child comes to understand that you will return and feels less anxious when you leave. Your child's earlier anxieties about being left may have faded away, but starting nursery and being plunged into an unfamiliar setting with new people can bring back these feelings.

Some degree of separation anxiety is normal when your child starts nursery, and you may be able to help to ease this by following some simple tips.

- Don't try to speed up the nursery settling-in process. If you work with nursery staff, gradually leaving your child for longer periods, there is far less chance of him becoming anxious.

- It can help a lot if he is always left with one member of staff at nursery, ideally his key worker. Sometimes this isn't possible if staff work shifts, but if he knows that there are one or two members of staff who are always there with him when you go, this can be beneficial.

- Never attempt to slip out without saying anything in order to avoid a scene. Always make sure that you say goodbye and tell your child when you will be back.

- Try to follow the same routine when you leave, so perhaps give him a hug, tell him you are going now and say when you will be back, give him a kiss and then leave. Don't make a big fuss about leaving as this will make him feel that there is something to be worried about.

- Make sure he has eaten a good breakfast before going to nursery, as if he is hungry or tired this can make him feel any separation anxiety more acutely.

- If he has a comforter, for example a blanket or specific toy that he is very attached to, you may want to consider letting him keep this with him at nursery. This is something you will want to think carefully about and should possibly discuss with staff first, too – finding someone else playing with his special teddy or a member of staff tidying it away with the other toys may be worse than not having it in the first place.

- You may want to consider leaving him with a small item of yours to help him feel secure that you will be coming back, but, again, do tell staff if you are going to leave him your scarf, for example, as otherwise they may think you have left it behind by mistake and put it away.

- Try to be sympathetic to how your child is feeling – if you seem impatient or act as if you feel he is being silly when he is upset, this can prolong the problem.

- When he comes home from nursery, try to spend some additional time together where you are solely focused on him and can give him all your attention.

Dealing with Your Own Concerns

You can help yourself feel happier about the early days by ensuring that you have built up a good relationship with the staff at the nursery. Make sure you know how to get in touch with them by phone or by email if you have any concerns and find out which method of communication they prefer. Check that you understand how they will communicate with you about what your child has been doing during the day. Many nurseries, particularly day nurseries, have a diary or day book system and if you know how you will be informed, it will be easier to have confidence in the nursery staff.

It will also help you feel better if you've made time to communicate any essential information about your child to the nursery staff. This isn't just vital medical information, such as details of allergies or health problems, but also more general tips about food that your child particularly dislikes or things that worry him, and any odd quirks that may help them care for your child more effectively. This is important because if he is given something to eat that he really can't stand on the very first day, or is read a story that you know always terrifies him, this can make a difference to the way he views the entire experience. If you know the staff are aware of anything that could really colour the way your child settles, this will help you to feel happier about leaving him in their care.

Final Preparations

Make sure that your child gets a good night's sleep the night before starting nursery – if necessary, get him ready for bed a little earlier than usual and spend longer on the bedtime story as you settle him to sleep. Although starting nursery in the morning may be at the forefront of your mind, try to make sure that you talk about some other things, too, so that the prospect of the next day doesn't start to feel overwhelming.

Think about what your child is going to wear for his first day at nursery, and get the clothes ready before he goes to bed. His outfit should be something comfortable and practical, which you don't mind getting dirty or splashed with paint. Make sure your child is confident about taking off whatever he is wearing and putting it on again and avoid clothes that have complicated fasteners. Don't make him wear something you know he doesn't like – he needs to feel confident. Imagine how you would feel if you had to wear an outfit you didn't like on your first day in a new job!

On the morning that your child is due to start nursery, leave yourself extra time to get yourselves ready. You don't want the first day to turn into a panicky rush, as this will create anxiety for you both. Make sure that your child has a proper breakfast before you leave, and something to drink, too. He may have a longer gap than he is used to before he eats again, and won't be able to enjoy activities properly if he is hungry or thirsty.

The First Day

The staff at the nursery will all be aware that this is your child's first day. They will make sure that they have things out that your child will enjoy, and should be ready to receive him in a cheerful, upbeat manner. They will show you where to leave his things, if you don't know already, and will be able to help encourage him to get involved in the first of the day's activities.

You may want to leave time to stay with your child for a brief period on the first day if the nursery encourages this, in order to give him some time to get interested in an activity. Then, once you can see that there is something he is going to enjoy, you can say goodbye.

Parents do sometimes worry about how to say goodbye to their child on that first day, and this can result in a long, drawn-out farewell, which may have more to do with their own needs than their child's. If you are hovering about and seeming uncertain about leaving your child, this will give him the message that there is something to worry about. It is best to try to be relatively brief, and not to draw out your goodbye as this can make things more difficult – it not only prolongs any potential difficulties, but can also stop your child being able to get on with getting absorbed in the toys and activities on offer.

You should always make sure you explain to your child that you will be back later to pick him up. Look cheerful and happy and tell him that you will look forward to hearing about all the exciting things he has done at nursery during the day. Don't attempt to avoid any possible trauma on the first day by slipping out when your child isn't looking. This may make things easier for you, but can be very upsetting for your child later when he realises that you have gone.

Children do sometimes cry when they are left for the first time, even if they haven't done so during the settling-in period. They will often be aware that this time it is for real. If your child does cry, try not to be too worried. Remember that it isn't unusual for children to cry on their first day and that it doesn't mean he is going to spend the entire day upset and in tears. Try to reassure him, give him a hug and a kiss and tell him that you are sure he is going to have a lovely time before handing him over to the nursery staff.

It is very upsetting for a parent to have to leave a child who is clearly upset and in tears in someone else's care as it goes against all your parental instincts. Try to remember that nursery staff are very experienced at dealing with this initial phase. They know that it is normally short-lived and that most children are perfectly all right as soon as their parents have gone and they can get involved in the day's activities.

Perhaps the most important message at this time is to ensure that you don't let your child see your distress. If he knows that you are upset, he is going to find it much harder to settle. Some nurseries may encourage you to sit outside the room for five minutes after leaving so that you can hear how quickly your child settles down. If you choose to do this, you must be careful not to let your child see you again before you leave as this could be very unsettling for him.

If you are going to feel worried, give the nursery a call once you get back home or to work to check how your child has been. Nurseries are just as used to anxious parents as they are anxious children; check beforehand who you should call and when might be a good time. Many parents will do this at first, so don't worry about appearing silly or overprotective. It's only natural to worry about your child when he first starts at nursery or playgroup, especially if neither of you has any previous experience of daycare.

You may find your first day apart from your child is hard for you, too. It may be difficult to stop thinking about him and what he might be doing throughout the day. If you are at work, you may find it hard to focus on your job for the first few days, particularly if you are returning to work for the first time since having your child, and this can come as a bit of a surprise.

Do rest assured that this will get easier with time as you both become familiar with your new daily pattern.

Make sure that you leave plenty of time to get to the nursery to pick your child up at the end of the day, and try to get there early if you can. It will help your child feel more confident about going to nursery if he knows that you are always there, ready and waiting for him, at the end of the day. If you are often the last parent to turn up and he has to wait as other children go off home with their parents, he may start to feel some unnecessary anxiety about whether you are going to be there to pick him up – this may colour his feelings about the whole nursery experience. If you can arrive early for the first few weeks at least, this will be worthwhile.

When you collect your child he will probably be very tired, as he will have spent the day in a new environment with new people doing different things. Try not to cross-examine him about every moment of his day. Of course, you will want to know what he has been doing and how he has reacted to it, but don't be worried if he doesn't want to talk about what he has done at all. This doesn't mean that he's had a bad day or hasn't enjoyed himself. He may not feel the need to tell you everything about his day as he may still be absorbing it all himself. The things that might be important to you – such as what he had for lunch and how much he ate – may feel less important to him than the type of trains they have in the nursery train set, so don't insist on answers to specific questions. If you are patient and give him time, he will be more forthcoming. Make sure you sound interested in anything he does say, admire any paintings or other craft work that he has brought home, but try to curb your natural instincts to want to know everything. The nursery staff should give you some feedback about your child's day, such as the activities he's enjoyed and the food he's eaten, either verbally or on a form.

Once you get home, stick to your normal routine for the rest of the day, evening and bedtime so that he can see that his life doesn't have to change entirely just because he is now at nursery. It can be a nice idea, if you collect your child early enough, to make sure that you have one of his favourite meals for supper as this will all help reinforce the positive messages that he is getting about his day. Give him as much time and attention as he seems to need, and you can make a point of telling him when he goes to bed how proud you are of him for settling in to nursery so well.

The Next Few Days

The first few days at nursery are all still part of the settling-in phase. Your child may be very tired, particularly if he is at nursery full-time, and this will be a huge change in his day-to-day life. He may be grumpy and irritable and it is important to try to keep this in context. He may be very happy during the day at nursery when he's engaged in play with others all day and having an exciting time, but once he gets back home with you and can relax, he may finally realise quite how tired he is and that's when any bad-tempered grumpiness can emerge.

Don't assume that a cross child isn't having a good time at nursery as sometimes it may be precisely because he's having such a busy and enjoyable day that he is tired and irritable once he gets back to the familiar territory of home.

Some children do take longer than others to adapt to nursery, and they may continue to be upset when they are left each morning. If you have to go through a tearful time every single day, this can become draining for you, too. It is extremely distressing to leave an unhappy child and it may be hard for you to concentrate properly during the day if you aren't sure that your child is all right. This sort of separation problem is usually short-lived, and a child who is distressed when a parent says goodbye is often to be found cheerfully careering around the room with friends just moments later. If you are having problems with this, discuss it with the nursery staff. They will be able to tell you how your child is once you have gone and how quickly he settles down to the rest of his day. They will also have a better idea whether this is just a normal part of settling in, or whether your child is genuinely finding it difficult to get used to nursery.

The vast majority of children do settle in fairly quickly, and even those who continue to have some problems at the moment of parting from their parents are often perfectly happy the rest of the time. There are, however, some children who do find it more of a struggle and who don't seem to be getting used to nursery at all. If you feel this may be the case, do discuss it with your child's key worker or other staff at the nursery but try to bear in mind that teething problems are quite normal, and that most children have to go through some kind of settling-in period.

Sometimes children who've had a fabulous first couple of days, and who seem to have settled in very well, will suddenly have a wobble a little way down the line when they realise that nursery or playgroup wasn't just for one day. This is just part of getting accustomed to a new phase of life and can be quite common, so don't assume the worst if your child seems to go off nursery after an initial honeymoon period. This can just be a simple matter of tiredness finally catching up with your child as well as the novelty wearing off, and you may need to be patient.

Parents sometimes find that a child who has been sleeping well, who seemed to sail through potty-training or who has always been very well-behaved experiences some degree of regression when he starts at nursery. It is easy to overlook how overwhelming an experience it can be for a young child; this is not only a complete change of environment, he also has to adjust to being with new adults and children and to learning new ways of doing things. It is not surprising that this can be stressful and can lead to regression. Your child may start being more clingy and revert to babyish behaviour, he may have toileting accidents, although he has been potty-trained for some time, and he may not want to go to bed as easily. The best way to deal with any of these issues is not to make too much of a fuss about them or to pay them too much attention, but to focus on praising good behaviour and reward this with more of your time and encouragement.

Dealing with Specific Problems

During each session at playgroup or nursery, your child will be facing many new or unfamiliar experiences and it can be small and seemingly insignificant issues that become problematic for him. It is inevitable that there will be some kind of teething problems along the way as your child adjusts to life in nursery. Whether it's a matter of getting over the phase of being tearful when you leave him in the morning or of concerns over specific things during the day, it can take a while for your child to get used to his new daily pattern. If he seems concerned about something at nursery or playgroup, you may need to be sensitive and patient in order to work out exactly where the problem lies.

Toileting accidents

One common problem for children of this age is using an unfamiliar toilet, and they may start having accidents when they have outgrown this at home. It can sometimes be a simple matter of being so absorbed in play that they forget to go to the toilet. It may be that they put off going at nursery because the sound of the hand-dryer scares them or because they find the toilet paper 'scratchy' – these things may sound silly or insignificant to an adult, but can so easily turn into real issues for young children.

If your child is having toileting accidents at nursery, talk to the staff as well as to your child to try to work out what might be causing the problem and whether there is any easy solution. It may be that a staff member needs to take your child to the toilet initially to ensure that no one puts the hand-dryer on unexpectedly, or that you need to put some tissues into his pocket so that he can use them instead of the 'scratchy' paper. Sometimes very small solutions like these can make all the difference to a child's overall happiness at nursery.

Regression is a common problem when children start nursery and toileting accidents may happen at home as well as at school. If your child does start having accidents at home, remind him what he should be doing by taking him to the potty or toilet, but focus on offering praise and encouragement when he does well rather than fussing too much about what has happened. Although regression can feel worrying for a parent, this is a common problem when children start at nursery and doesn't usually last long.

Eating

Your child may not like certain foods, or may not like the way in which they are prepared. Talk to the nursery staff if your child is having particular concerns about eating something as it is usually possible to ensure that a child isn't given something that he really dislikes. It is also worth talking to the staff about their policy around mealtimes as children sometimes feel pressured into eating things that they really don't like at nursery. Do keep in mind, however, that children often quite cheerfully eat things at nursery that they wouldn't touch at home. Unless he seems concerned about having to eat things at nursery, don't automatically assume, for example, that it was a problem for your vegetable-phobic child to eat a plate of green beans and peas at nursery! The key here is to ensure you have a good communication channel with the staff, and in particular with your child's key worker, so that you can clear up any problems that arise quickly and efficiently.

Friendships

This is another problem area that can cause more worries for parents than for children. It is only natural for a parent to be concerned if their child doesn't seem to be making friends or to be establishing any friendship groups at nursery, but children of this age are still building their social skills and won't necessarily have friends in the way that they will do as they get older. If your child is really interested in some of the activities at nursery, he may well mention these far more than he talks about other children. He may not seem to have any particularly close friends and may only ever talk about the girl who is very naughty or the boy who has an allergy, as these may be the things that have struck him about particular children. If pressed, young children may well say that they don't have any friends at all or that they don't ever play with the other children, but in such cases it is always worth checking this with the nursery staff before worrying about it as they may present a very different picture of your child's friendships from an adult observer's point of view.

It is important to keep in mind that your child is looking at everything from his own perspective and, although it is important to listen, you also need to assess what your child is telling you. Children live much more in the moment than adults do, and will sometimes tell you things that sound worrying to a parent, particularly around friendships and the way that other children treat them, but may have completely forgotten about them by the next day. It is always a matter of getting the balance right between listening to what your child says in a sympathetic and understanding way and assessing the significance of what he has told you.

There are some ways you can help your child to feel more confident about socialising at nursery:

- **Having playdates:** The most obvious way to ensure your child is familiar with the other children in his nursery class is to have playdates with them. If you know other parents already this is easier to arrange, but it is worth making the effort to try to invite other children over anyway. Seeing one other child without the rest of the group on familiar home territory may help your child feel more in control.

- **Attending groups:** Ask other parents if their children attend any other local groups, such as music or ballet classes. Seeing children from nursery outside the classroom can help to establish social relationships.

- **Learning to share:** Make sure that your child understands about the need to share toys and take turns when you play with him at home. He will find it far easier to play with others at nursery if he understands these concepts.

Shyness

Some children are more naturally gregarious than others, and not all children want to be the centre of attention at nursery, but you may worry if you feel your child is not joining in or is reluctant to play with others. It can take a while for children to settle into nursery and feel confident in their new environment, so there is no cause for concern unless this persists beyond the first few weeks. If staff report that your child isn't wanting to join in or talk to others, it is a good idea to talk to him about this without making it into a big issue. You may find there is a specific reason for his shyness, which you can address. If this is not the case, there are some tips to help him overcome this:

- The most important advice is not to label your child as 'shy'. Once a child has a label it can be very hard to lose it – and he may find it much harder to join in if he thinks he has a reason not to.

- Do show your child that you empathise with his feelings. If possible, tell him about occasions when you felt shy as a child.

- Try to encourage him to spend more time with others by inviting children from nursery or other friends over for playdates. It will help to break the ice if you have a planned activity to do with the children when the friend arrives, such as baking cupcakes together, so that your child doesn't feel pressured.

- Ask at your local library if they can recommend any children's books about overcoming shyness (see page 201 for recommendations) and read them together.

- You may want to practise social skills through role-play with dolls or teddies, making sure that your child knows how to introduce himself to others and to make conversation.

- Remember that children learn behaviour from adults. If you are quite shy yourself, acting in a more chatty, sociable way in front of your child when you are with others can help.

Aggression

One of the most upsetting problems at nursery for a parent is discovering that your child has hurt another child, or has been aggressive or violent. A one-off episode may be excitement or over-exuberance leading to rough behaviour, but regular episodes of hitting, biting, pinching, and rudeness, aggression and violence towards nursery staff or other children must be addressed.

Some children have phases of pinching or biting, and it may be a matter of establishing that this is unacceptable behaviour. As with any kind of bad behaviour at this age, focusing on praising good behaviour and not rewarding bad with too much attention is most effective.

More general aggression and violence is likely to have some kind of trigger and it is important to look not only at what is happening during the day at nursery, but also what is happening the rest of the time at home. Lack of sleep, frustration, insecurity and attention-seeking can all lead to aggressive behaviour, and you may want to think about possible triggers – for example, a new baby in the family tying in with a start at nursery may be making your child feel that his position is being usurped.

If your child does not have clear boundaries at home, or if you are inconsistent in the way that you deal with bad behaviour, it is going to be more difficult for him to accept rules and boundaries at nursery. The nursery will have policies for dealing with bad behaviour and you should make sure that what you do at home and what happens at nursery are consistent and that any potential triggers for bad behaviour are being addressed.

Special Educational Needs

If you are aware that your child will need some extra attention at nursery because he has some special needs, whether these are physical, behavioural or purely educational, you may worry about how he will cope. All nurseries should have policies in place to explain how they ensure that the needs of such children are met, and there should also be a dedicated member of staff who deals with this, called the Special Educational Needs Coordinator or SENCO. A child with special needs should be able to attend nursery in just the same way as any other child, and if you know that your child has special educational needs you should liaise with the SENCO at the nursery of your choice.

Depending on the nature of the problem, the SENCO will discuss with you the level of support needed for your child, which may vary from an action plan involving a little extra help at times in the classroom to support from outside specialists and an assessment and statement of special educational needs. All the staff in the nursery should be aware of your child's needs, and ensuring that your child is receiving all the additional support he is entitled to will be an ongoing process.

Sometimes learning difficulties begin to become apparent at nursery, and it may only be at this stage or later that the first signs of a difficulty begin to appear. If you suspect that a child who is already at nursery is not progressing as you would expect or is having some kind of problem, the first person to talk to would be his key worker who can refer you to the SENCO.

Your Child's Development at Nursery

Within a relatively short time you may wonder why you ever worried about your child settling in at nursery. He may seem so much an old hand as you watch him racing around the playground or settling down to games with friends that you can scarcely remember how anxious you were at the start. Of course, there will be issues that arise now and again during your child's time at nursery as he grows older and his needs change. It is important to maintain your communication channels with the nursery so that you always know who to talk to if any problems arise. Your child's key worker is the most likely point of contact, but sometimes staff members move on and his key worker may change during the time he is at nursery.

You should also be kept up to date with your child's progress and development during his time at nursery. Each nursery will have an established system of reporting back to parents, and it may be that you get a report each term or annually, or that you are encouraged to go in for a chat with the teacher to discuss progress. It is important to make time to follow up any opportunities to meet the nursery staff, as they might want to raise specific issues with you.

Most nurseries focus on play-based learning and will not begin any kind of formal education with your child. Learning numbers and letters will usually be approached in a very relaxed and informal manner, and your child will not be aware of any kind of pressure to learn. Some nurseries do adopt a more formal approach, but it is generally accepted that children of this age learn better through play.

Don't worry if your child seems slow to get to grips with letters or numbers. It is often said that children learn at different paces, and parents can assume this to mean that those who learn more slowly will continue to be slower throughout their educational lives. In fact, this is far from the truth and children who learn later often learn faster, so things even out as they get older.

Don't be tempted to compare your child with others who may seem to be learning more quickly and be careful not to let your child pick up on any sense of comparison with his peers at this stage. If your child is interested, you can spend some time on games that involve letters and numbers at home, but don't push this if he clearly doesn't want to do it. This doesn't mean he isn't going to be bright, it just means it's not the right time. Trying to cram formal learning into a child who isn't ready for it can be off-putting and risks setting a template for future problems. If you are guided by your child's level of interest, you will probably find that your progress is far speedier once he wants to learn himself.

Of course, if you have any concerns at all about your child's development you should talk to the nursery staff – but it is quite likely that they will have approached you themselves if they have spotted any educational problems. Children develop at different rates and in different ways, so the child who is an early reader may not have such well-developed social skills and the child who is clearly very creative may be slower to learn numbers. Just in the way that adults are different, so too are children. Some parents can be competitive about their children, but it is always best to try to avoid getting drawn into unhealthy comparisons.

The Path Ahead

As time goes on, you will gradually start to see more of the benefits of nursery or playgroup as your child grows in confidence. You will see how his social skills develop and how he becomes more at ease in group settings. You will notice his growing independence as he does things at home that you would have done for him without thinking in the past. Nursery will become part of his daily routine and he will no longer think of it as something new or different, but just another part of his life.

You will find that your child's horizons broaden through the time he has spent at nursery as he develops new interests and makes new friends. It can also be beneficial for you as a parent, as you will meet others with children of the same age and will establish new groups of friends who can provide a supportive network.

It is perhaps looking to the future that you will notice the biggest advantages of the time spent at nursery as your child moves on to start school. He will have spent time away from you with groups of others of his age, he will be used to sitting and listening, he will have more developed social skills and will have learnt how to interact with new adults and with other children of his own age. Moving on to the next stage of life will be a big adventure, but one that he is fully equipped to handle.

Case History: Sam – Starting Nursery

I worked full-time when Sam was a baby and we had a nanny. He was nearly three when I got pregnant, and I was going to take an extended maternity leave so I thought it would be a good time for Sam to start a couple of sessions of nursery. I went to see a local day nursery that had a good reputation.

I took Sam with me for a look around, and he was very taken with all the activities on offer. They had an outside play area with a garden where the children were growing vegetables and sunflowers, and dedicated areas inside for different activities. They said Sam could have two mornings if he could start right away, but otherwise we'd have to go on the waiting list. He seemed to like it, so I went for him starting right away.

They said there would be a two-week settling-in period, but they expected parents to try to leave their child on the first day, just for a short period. Sam had only ever been with us and his nanny, and hadn't spent a lot of time with other children, but they advised me to try leaving for 10 minutes or so once he seemed happy. He loved all the toys, and after about an hour I gave him a kiss and said goodbye. He didn't understand that I was going at first, but when he realised he ran across the room after me and clung on to my leg and started crying, so I didn't go anywhere at all.

The next time I felt I had to leave him for at least a little while, and one of the staff took him off to read him a story when I said goodbye. He started crying as I left and I could hear him wailing as I walked down the road. I went and sat in the car and watched the minutes going past. After about 10 minutes, I couldn't bear it any more and I went back. He'd stopped crying but looked so sad.

I left for about an hour the next week, and he cried again, although he was better when I came back. The staff kept reassuring me it was common for children to react this way when they first started, but I felt horrible leaving him. By the time we had his first proper paid session, he was meant to be there all morning until after lunch. I took him in and the staff had to peel him off me. It was upsetting for us both. I could hear him crying and crying as I walked out, and I didn't enjoy the morning at all. When I got back at lunchtime, he was sitting with all the others listening to a story and he looked fine. The staff said he'd only cried for a little while, but he'd been so upset when I left I couldn't believe it was true.

He cried every single time I left him for the first few weeks, but when I went to collect him, he'd be playing outside with the others really happily. He talked about nursery a lot at home, and it was all positive, but it didn't make it any easier to leave him. I talked about it to the staff, and they said he'd stop crying within a few minutes of me going. In the end, his key worker told me to go and sit in the staff room instead of walking out of the front door when I left so I could hear. He was crying just as usual when I left, and it really was a few minutes after I'd 'gone' that he stopped.

I think just doing a couple of mornings at nursery made it harder for him to adjust to me leaving because there were such long periods in between. When I went back to work, he started doing more sessions and it seemed to make it much better. I also wonder whether he felt the new baby was going to take his place in the family and whether it wasn't the best time for him to be having another big change in his life.

3

Before Your Child Starts School

Even if your child has been at nursery for years, the move to primary school will be a big step forward. It is a time of change for your child and you all as a family, and you will want to be sure that you have found the right school where he will be able to flourish and achieve his potential. You will also want to do all you can to prepare your child and yourself for the early days at school to ensure that this proves to be a happy and positive experience that will set your child off on the right foot for his educational future.

In England and Wales, the school year begins in September and children who will be five before the end of that academic year will join school either at the start or sometimes later on during that year. In Scotland the system is slightly different as the school year begins in August and children join the school when they are between the age of four-and-a-half and five-and-a-half depending on their birthday. They can join the school at the start of the year in August if they are going to be five before the end of February. The first year in schools in England and Wales is called Reception, while in Scotland it is Primary 1. In Northern Ireland, children start school at four, and the first year of school is Year 1. In the private education system, children leaving nursery will move into a pre-prep school that usually caters for children between the ages of 4–7, and they will then move on to a preparatory school.

Choosing the Right School

In some areas, there may not be a choice of primary schools – for example, if you live in a rural area and there is only one option within a reasonable distance. This can make life much easier as all the local children will go to the same school, and there won't be any fuss or worry about whether your child will get into the school of your choice.

For most parents, there will be a choice of at least a couple of possible primary schools and maybe many more, particularly if you are also considering independent schools. There are some key factors that you should take into consideration when you are deciding which school would be best for your child:

- **Location:** The location of a school and the daily journey to get there should be a key factor in your decision-making process. Young children do get tired, and if you are considering a school some distance away because it appears to be a 'better' school, you should think carefully about the journey before making a final decision. A local school is part of the local community, and being able to walk to school and having friends who live nearby can help to make going to school more fun for children. A long car journey every day can be tiring and it may make things more difficult for you if your child's friends all live some distance away. Your chances of getting a place for your child at a state primary school which isn't near to your home may be limited, as most popular schools are only able to offer places to children who live close by.

- **Other parents' opinions:** It can be difficult not to be influenced by what other parents are saying locally about the options. In many areas, there is one favoured school, which often becomes much harder to get into than others and parents inevitably assume that this must be the best school. Of course you should talk to other parents and listen to their views and experiences, but remember that what is best for one child is not always best for another. It is important to go into the process with an open mind if you can and try to make your own judgements.

- **Think about your child:** It's easy to be swayed by what other parents think, but what is right for their child may not be right for yours. Some children flourish in big, boisterous schools with lots going on, while others may feel far more secure in a smaller, more traditional school. Think about your child's character and his needs, and this will help you to assess how the different options available would suit him.

- **Think about your family:** Sometimes the needs of your whole family come into play when you're considering schools for your child. It may be that the location of a certain school would be far easier for you to manage if you are going in one direction to work, or that you have relatives or friends with children at the school who will share the school run. It's important to bear these things in mind as they can influence the smooth running of family life, which will make a difference to your child.

- **Open days:** Most schools run open days for prospective parents where you can look around and see what you think of the school. Going to an open day is one of the best ways to get an idea of what the school is like and whether it would suit your child. You will find a list of what to look out for on an open day on page 86.

- **School website:** Not all primary schools have websites, but many do and looking at these can give you more information about the schools you are considering. There will be details about the school itself as well as pictures, and school newsletters are often published online, too – these can give an insight into the some of the activities that go on. You can often find out about after-school clubs, school trips and special projects from the website. School term dates may be listed here, too. Check whether the school produces a prospectus, which may be available directly from the school or downloaded from the website.

- **School policies:** Some primary schools publish their policies on their websites, but all will have set ways for dealing with issues such as child protection, bullying, behaviour and attendance. If you cannot find any particular policies on the website which you would like to see, you can ask the school directly.

- **Inspection reports:** Schools are regularly inspected to ensure that they are maintaining the required standards, and these reports are available online for anyone who is interested in reading them. They give a good overall picture of the school as inspectors spend time in the school visiting classrooms, watching teachers at work and seeing how well pupils are being taught. Schools are then graded according to this assessment. Most will be satisfactory, good or even outstanding, but if a school is not doing sufficiently well it may be served with a notice to improve in some areas or put into special measures, which means that urgent changes are needed.

- **League tables:** If you live in an area where primary schools are assessed according to the children's educational achievements, this can seem a logical way to distinguish between different schools. It is important to keep this in context, though. Once a school becomes desirable, it tends to fill with children whose parents are keen for them to perform well and it is far easier for schools to achieve high results with these children. It may be that a school that doesn't appear to do as well is actually making far more of an impact on children's learning. The other thing to bear in mind is that some schools spend far more time than others practising for the tests and that these don't necessarily reflect the children's overall academic attainment. You may want to look at the results, but think carefully before making judgements based on league tables alone.

- **After-school or breakfast clubs:** If you are working full-time, you need to think about how you will manage at either end of the short school day. Many schools have breakfast clubs in the morning and after-school clubs in the afternoon, but it doesn't necessarily follow that there will be places available. There may be a waiting list if the demand is very high so make sure you have the most up-to-date information about this. If there won't be a place, or if the school cannot offer provision before and after school, you may need to consider looking for additional childcare to cover these hours.

- **State school or independent school:** There is little more divisive for parents than deciding whether to pay for a child's education privately, and many people have strong views about this one way or the other. This is very much an individual decision and you will want to weigh up the advantages and disadvantages for your child and your family. Although many independent schools offer bursaries and scholarships for very bright children at senior level, this is far less common at primary school level, so you will need to bear in mind that you are unlikely to get help from the school with the fees and you will be making a commitment for some years, unless you intend to move your child into the state system at a later date.

Independent schools can set their own curriculum, but still have to be registered with the government and they are still regularly inspected. They can usually offer smaller class sizes, and other benefits may include more extra-curricular activities and sports, better facilities and academic results. Schools within the independent sector vary hugely, though, and it is important not to make any assumptions about what a school can or cannot offer simply because it is in the independent sector. Visit the school yourself before making a decision.

If you are choosing an independent school for your child, you will want to think about your longer-term plans. If you are planning to keep your child in the independent system for senior school, too, you should find out about the destinations of leavers from the prep school you are considering, and the numbers of pupils who have been successful in the entrance exams for schools you think you may want your child to attend at senior level.

Some senior schools have a prep and pre-prep department, and this may make the transition to the senior school easier. If you are choosing an independent school with the aim of your child moving on to the senior department of the same school, do find out whether children are automatically offered places if they move up from the prep school, and if not how many children would usually get in.

Within the state system, there are a variety of different types of school that you may want to consider. The majority of local primary schools will be community schools that are run by the local authority, but you may find that some of the schools in your area operate differently. There are many faith schools that are associated with a particular religion, most often the Church of England or the Roman Catholic Church. Faith schools are very much like any other primary school, but they are able to teach pupils about their religion and they may give priority to those who have attended their church regularly when they are admitting new children into the school. Free schools are fairly new and may be set up by groups such as businesses, charities or parents. Although free schools are state schools with funding from the government, they have more freedom and don't have to follow the national curriculum or employ qualified teachers. If you are considering a free school, you will want to investigate how the school differs from other local schools. Most academy schools are within the secondary sector, but there are now some primary school academies. Academy schools are state schools but they are often sponsored by a business or charity, and they get state funding from central government rather than the local council. Like the free schools, they can set their own rules about certain aspects of school life and don't have to follow the national curriculum.

What to look for on a school open day

During an open day, most schools will give you a tour around the buildings and grounds and this may be done in groups or individually. Sometimes the head teacher will lead the tour, but responsibility may be handed over to another teacher or even some older pupils. There may also be a talk from the head teacher or a chance to chat to members of staff and ask questions. It is useful to jot down anything you particularly want to find out in advance so that you don't forget when you're looking around. If the school has a website, take a look at this before you visit as it may highlight other issues that you want to find out about.

Parents sometimes feel that they aren't quite sure what they ought to be looking for during a visit, but one of the most important reasons for an open day is to get a feel for the school and to see whether you think it would be right for your child and your family. There are some key points that you may want to consider:

- Do the children seem happy and involved in classes, or do they look bored and uninterested? How do they interact with one another? And how do the staff interact with the pupils?

- What facilities are there at the school? You may want to find out about any specific facilities for sport, music, drama, art and IT, for example.

- What is the playground like? Is it an imaginative space for the children? Does it look as if the children are enjoying the space when they are outside?

- Is there lots of the children's work on the walls? Does it look as if only the 'best' work has been selected or does it represent a range of different abilities?

- Ask about the staff to pupil ratio. Are teaching assistants employed full-time to help in classes? What is the staff turnover? How many teachers are newly qualified? Ideally, you would want to see a balance between teachers who are new to the profession and those who are more experienced.

- How much focus is given to music, art, drama and sport in the school?

- What extra-curricular activities are available? Can the children learn instruments or get involved in sports clubs?

- Are any specific teaching methods used in the school?

- What are the policies for dealing with bullying and bad behaviour, and for rewarding those who do well?

- Ask about the school's homework policy and see whether this matches your own views as to how much work children should be expected to do at home.

- Are there regular school trips and outings?

- Find out how your child's progress would be monitored and how you will be kept informed of this.

- You may want to take your child with you to open days. Children see things in a completely different way, and while you are focusing on academic achievements, they may notice things that you haven't even thought about.

- If your child has any special educational needs, check how the school would deal with this and what support would be available.

- Is there a parent-teacher association or family society? How involved is it in the school's day-to-day life?

- Each school does have a slightly different ambience, and you shouldn't ignore your first impressions or the initial overall feel of the school. You are looking for an environment that you feel will suit your child and he will find stimulating. Can you see your child at the school and do you think he'd be happy there?

- How well organised was the open day? This can give you an idea of how efficiently the school operates.

Getting a Place

It's all very well deciding which school you like, but you will also need to secure a place for your child there. In some areas, this won't be a problem but in others some primary schools are oversubscribed and not everyone who wants a place will get in.

Most primary schools prioritise children according to how close they live to the school. Although school catchment areas usually alter slightly from year to year, you can get a rough idea of how likely it is that your child will get a place from how far children have lived from the school in previous years. Siblings are usually given priority above distance, so in a small school you may find that younger brothers and sisters can make up a hefty percentage of the intake.

Faith schools operate different admissions policies as they will take children who come from families who show religious commitment. If you are considering a faith school, you may need a letter from your vicar or priest to confirm that you have been going to church regularly over a period of time.

Sometimes, getting into a particular school can become almost an obsession and occasionally parents do go to extremes just to get into a particular school; they may move house and uproot their families, rent a house close to a particularly desirable school or suddenly start attending church in order to get a child into a faith school. Think carefully before resorting to such measures, as generally the difference between schools is not so great that it would merit a complete upheaval for the entire family.

State school applications are made through your local authority in the UK, and they will have details of an individual school's admissions policies. It is vital to find out about the key dates in the admissions process: what the deadline is for applications and when you will find out whether you have got a place at the school of your choice. You will usually be able to apply online or on a form, and will be able to list a number of schools in order of preference. It's a good idea to start looking at schools during the year before you will be applying to ensure you are ready to make your choices in time for the deadline.

If you don't get into the school of your choice, you can appeal but in order to win an appeal you would have to not only demonstrate that the school in question was the only place suitable for your child but also that the admissions policy had been wrongly applied in some way. You can also go on the waiting list for the school of your choice. Places often do come up in between the first offers and the starting date, so don't despair if you are on a waiting list. Parents sometimes find that they accept a place elsewhere in the interim, and that they end up finding that their second choice school suits them just as well as the one they'd originally wanted, if not even better.

If you are applying to an independent school, you and your child may be interviewed and your child may be given some kind of assessment. This will usually be to see how ready the children are to learn and to get an idea of their concentration and language skills. You should check with the school what the assessment includes and try to talk to other parents who have children at the school, as this will give you a clearer idea of what might be expected of your child. Not all schools have an assessment, as some are happy to take any children who want to come to the school in the early years. You will probably be asked to pay a deposit in advance. Oversubscribed independent schools may have waiting lists for places.

What You Need to Know Before Your Child Starts School

Once you've been offered a place at a school for your child and have accepted it, you will probably receive more information about the school, covering both policies and practicalities. It will detail the arrangements for starting, as well as giving information about school timings and dates. You should also be given details of who to contact at the school if your child is ill or is unable to attend for any other reason. If you have any queries about things that aren't covered in the information you receive, you can always contact the school in advance to ensure you feel properly prepared.

You will want to make sure that you are aware of any uniform or dress code regulations. Where there is a uniform, the information should include details of where to purchase it. If you need to order the uniform in advance, do this sooner rather than later so that you know your child will have all he needs on his first day. Getting school uniform can be exciting for a young child, so try to encourage his sense of enjoyment about this by showing him the uniform and letting him try it on. You should also be clear about any special kit that is needed for PE, and you may need to buy a PE bag for your child. Most primary schools have book bags and these are usually provided or can be purchased from the school itself.

Don't forget to label all your child's clothing clearly and to show him the labels so that he can recognise his own name in his things. You can buy iron-on named labels or ones that clip into clothes, or if you prefer you can just use a marker pen on the existing labels in his clothing. It's particularly important to make sure you label all items of uniform.

There should also be information about meals, and you may need to decide whether you would prefer your child to have a school lunch or whether you are happy to provide a packed lunch. Some children love having school dinners and the food provided has generally improved in recent years, but others prefer the familiarity of food from home. You may find that once your child starts school he will change his mind about having school dinners or packed lunch depending on what most of his friends are doing, so be prepared for this.

The policies part of the information that you are sent may include some kind of Home-School agreement, which parents are asked to sign. It is a form of contract between the parents and the school and it usually explains the school's aims, values and responsibilities and also details what the school expects from parents and pupils. Parents may be asked to commit to ensuring that their child arrives at school on time, in suitable clothing, to support their child's learning, to attend parents' evenings and to work in partnership with the school on issues such as behaviour. It may detail what is expected of children, such as behaving kindly and being helpful, taking care of school equipment and respecting others. In return the school will promise to care for your child's safety and to help him to achieve his full potential by providing a balanced curriculum and meeting his needs. The agreement may also mention that the staff will keep you informed about school matters and about your child's individual progress.

Most of what is expected of the children is in fairly simple, straightforward language and talking this through with your child may help reassure him that he will be safe and looked after when he starts school. You don't need to make a big issue about it, but just explain that now he is old enough to start school, he is also old enough to make sure he behaves properly while he is there.

Preparing Your Child for School Emotionally

Starting school feels like a period of huge change for you and your child, and you will want to do all you can to prepare him for this new phase of life. Some children feel quite anxious about starting school but others seem to take it all in their stride. It will undoubtedly be easier for a child who has already been at nursery, particularly if the nursery is part of the primary school he is moving on to, and if he already has friends, neighbours or siblings at the school.

Positive attitudes

You can do a lot to help your child by adopting a positive attitude towards the school and by stressing that going to school will be an interesting and enjoyable experience. Focus on some of the elements of primary education that you know your child will enjoy and try to emphasise these when you are discussing school, but be careful not to raise expectations that every day will be spent playing football or drawing!

You may want to talk to your child about your own time at primary school and how much you enjoyed it, or about other older children he knows who are at school. Talk about some of the things that they've done at school that you know might appeal to your child to encourage him to feel enthusiastic.

If you didn't manage to get your child into your first choice school, try not to let him be aware of this. Children do pick up on far more than you might expect, and even if you feel less than enthusiastic about the school yourself, you should be careful not to transmit this to your child. If he was aware of your original choice and asks why he isn't going there after all, you can explain that too many children wanted to go there and that he was fortunate to get a place at another lovely school, which will be just as much fun.

It can be difficult if children aren't going to the same school as friends from nursery or playgroup. Your child may not be that aware of where other people are going, but this can sometimes worry those who want to be with a familiar group of friends. If you are able to seek out any other children who will be going to the same school, this may help your child to feel more confident.

Of course, you want to do all that you can to foster a positive attitude to school, but do make sure you keep it in perspective. The idea of your child finally starting his education may be a far bigger deal for you than it is for him. Don't forget to talk about other things than starting school, otherwise your good intentions may be counter-productive. Your child may start to suspect that the emphasis you are putting on starting school must mean that there is something he ought to be concerned about.

Books

There are lots of children's books that specifically deal with starting school (see page 201 for recommendations) and it is a good idea to get some of these from your local library or bookshop so you can look at them with your child. Books about starting school often address some of the worries that children may have but will usually end on a happy, upbeat note with a child realising that school is actually quite good fun. Children will absorb the messages from these books, and it is well worth doing a bit of research to find books that you feel your child will be able to relate to.

Information

If your child has lots of questions about school, try to answer them as best you can. Children sometimes worry about all kinds of odd things that aren't at all the issues that an adult would consider, but it is vital to be patient and to address these however insignificant they may seem to you. Make sure you know about the school's daily routine yourself so that you can talk to your child about this. Explain what will happen during the day as this will all be new to your child and he may not understand things such as playtimes or lunch breaks. You may find that doing some role-play games focusing on school and school activities will help him to feel more confident. You may prefer to use puppets for role-play games, or you can act them out with your child yourself. You may want to try taking the role of the teacher and calling out a register, which your child has to answer, or reading him stories as his teacher and asking questions about them – alternatively, letting your child play the role of the teacher for you and/ or his toys can be a good way of helping him to feel more familiar with the idea of school.

Knowing the school

If you are able to familiarise your child with his new school, this can be very helpful and there may be a number of opportunities in the lead-up to his first day. Schools often have some kind of induction day and if there is a chance to visit as part of a settling-in process, do take this up. There may be school events, such as school fairs or fetes, that you can attend and this will help familiarise your child with his new school. You may want to do the journey to school together a few times so that your child is familiar with the route and with the buildings and local area. Going on a walk past the school and looking in at the classrooms and the playground can give an opportunity to discuss some of the enjoyable things he will be able to do there. Being familiar with the school buildings, playground and the local area can help to make the first day seem less strange.

Shopping

If your child is going to need any new items for school, for example uniform, a PE kit, lunch bag or pencil case, then you can take him on a special shopping trip to choose the items that he will need. This can help to build a sense of excitement about starting school, especially if he is allowed to select the items himself.

New friends

If you can, do try to make contact with other families who have children who will be joining the school at the same time. Try to arrange a few playdates, or to meet up in the park or playground once or twice, so that your child will recognise one or two familiar faces on the first day. If you don't know any other families who have children who will be starting at the same time, it's still a good idea to try to get together with other families you know who have older children at the school. Knowing that your child is familiar with someone who is already there will make a huge difference to your child and to you on his first day.

Crowds

For a small child, the crowded atmosphere in a school playground with lots of older children racing about can feel daunting at first. You may want to take your child out to some busy places so that he doesn't feel too worried by the playground. Local places that can get crowded with children are a good idea; perhaps a playground or the local swimming pool. This may help your child to feel less worried about being in a crowded, noisy atmosphere surrounded by lots of other people.

Toilets

One thing children can really worry about is the school toilets. They will probably offer less privacy than your facilities at home, and may feel strange at first to your child. It's a good idea to encourage your child to use public toilets when you are out and about to ensure he doesn't feel uncomfortable about the school facilities. Children do sometimes have an occasional toileting accident (see page 65) when they first start school, and you may want to mention to your child in passing that this can happen sometimes and that teachers are used to it and are very understanding.

Food

Some parents prefer to give their child a packed lunch when they first start school, feeling that familiar food may be helpful, but others prefer them to have a cooked meal at lunchtime and opt for school dinners. If your child is having packed lunch, talk to him about what he'd like for lunch and ensure he has things that you know he enjoys. Buying a new lunchbox and water bottle that he has chosen himself can make him more enthusiastic about the idea of eating his packed lunch. If your child is going to be having school dinners, you may want to take him out to lunch once or twice, with friends or to a cafe, before he starts school. Don't worry too much if your child tends to be picky about food at home, as peer pressure can encourage fussy eaters to try all kinds of things they'd never normally touch at home once they get to school. Don't forget that children are often quite excited for the first few days and sometimes may not be able to eat as much as they normally would at home.

Young children can find it hard to get right through from breakfast to lunch without a snack, and some schools do provide fruit at break time. If you think this may be an issue for your child, find out in advance whether the school provides snacks or whether it is possible for your child to bring in his own snack for break time.

Daily routines

It can be a good idea to practise some of the new daily routines before your child starts school, particularly when it comes to getting up and ready for school in the morning. If your child has been at nursery or playgroup before, this won't be so hard, but children who have been at home with one carer, whether it's a parent or a nanny, have sometimes got used to a fairly laid-back start to the day and may need a little practice at getting up, dressed and having breakfast in time to set off for school. You may also want to think about the routine during the day, perhaps having lunch at the same time that your child does at school. Don't forget that the first few weeks of school are going to be very tiring, and you may want to bring bedtime forward a little in the weeks leading up to the first day so that you can be sure that your child is getting plenty of sleep.

Saying goodbye

If your child has never been at nursery, the thought of you going off and leaving him for a day once he starts school may be very worrying. It's a good idea to practise leaving him for short periods of time with friends or family, and to develop a familiar way of parting – so you may always give him a kiss and cuddle and tell him you love him and when you will be back. If he is used to this, it will be far easier for you to use this method when you leave him on the first day at school. Do check with the school whether you will be able to go into the classroom with him initially and how long you will be allowed to stay, so that you can prepare him by explaining what to expect.

Younger siblings

One of the things that can make starting school difficult for a child is the idea that a younger sibling will now have the parent or carer to himself. When you are talking about school in the weeks before your child starts, stress how envious his younger sibling will be, how he wishes he could start school, too, and how bored he will be stuck at home without his older sibling as a playmate.

Home time

Make sure your child understands what time the school day finishes and knows who will be there to collect him. It's always a good idea to be there early for the first few weeks at least. Some schools have a gradual settling-in process, so children may not do the full school day for the first day or for the first week. Make sure your child understands exactly what will happen before he starts so he isn't worried about this.

Developing Practical Skills for School

Parents are often worried about their children having the right academic preparation for starting school, and may focus on concerns about teaching letters, numbers or basic reading skills. In fact, it is often far more important at this stage to focus on the practical skills that your child will need for school as these will prove far more important during his early days. It's easy to underestimate how much difference skills such as being able to do up shoes or get undressed can make to a small child starting school.

Toilet-training

By this stage, most children have been successfully toilet-trained, but some may be anxious about using public toilets and may still have occasional accidents when they get absorbed in activities and forget to go to the toilet. It's important to do all you can to encourage your child to feel comfortable about using the toilet at school and making sure he has used public toilets now and again will help. If you pay a visit to the school with your child before he starts, make sure you include the toilets in your tour even if you have to request this. It will help to deal with any concerns. Make sure that your child knows who to ask if he needs to go to the toilet and where to go. Some schools do try to encourage children right from the start to use the toilet at break or lunchtime in order to ensure that class time isn't interrupted, but most adopt a more flexible approach when children first join the school. If your child has had any specific problems with toilet-training in the past, it is worth informing the teacher.

Some children have toileting accidents when they first start at school and the teachers will be used to it, so make sure your child is aware of this. Don't use school as a threat if your child has an occasional accident at home – for example by saying, 'You won't be able to have accidents once you start school,' as this is more likely to make him worry and will be counter-productive.

Dressing and undressing

Children will usually have to get changed for PE lessons at school, and it is a good idea to allow your child to practise getting in and out of his PE kit himself. It is often tempting to continue to dress a small child who can take a long time to dress himself, especially if you are in a hurry in the mornings, but do resist this as it is important that he feels confident about dressing himself. Make sure he is able to put his coat on properly and take it off, too. It's easy to assume that your child can do this, but you may actually always zip up his coat or do up the buttons without thinking about it!

Get him to practise taking his shoes off, putting them on and doing them up, too. Velcro fasteners are a good idea for small children who can struggle with buckles or laces.

Generally, it's a good idea to put your child in comfortable clothes that you aren't too worried about when he begins school, and to choose items that he can get on and off himself. Items that are easy to pull on with as few zips and buttons as possible tend to work best.

Knowing about himself

It is unlikely that your child will ever find himself alone outside school without you, but knowing how to explain who he is and where he lives can be essential. Make sure that your child knows how to respond if someone asks him his name, and knowing his address and who his parents are can also be very helpful in school. If your child is good with numbers, you may want to encourage him to try to memorise your phone number, too. He needs to understand when it is appropriate to disclose this information to friends, family, teachers or people in authority, and when it might not be right to tell strangers this kind of personal information. This can be a fine balance with young children, and you don't want to worry him unnecessarily but even at this age you can explain that it would not be right for him to get into a car with a stranger.

Mealtimes

Sometimes parents or carers give their child far more help at mealtimes than they realise; for example, you may cut up your child's food, wipe his face or even feed him without really being aware that he isn't used to dealing with mealtimes without help. Do let him get on with meals without trying to help or interfere, even if you fear it will mean that he won't eat as well as he does when you help him. It will help your child if he is confident about getting through mealtimes without help once he starts school.

If your child is having school lunches, he may need to queue up in a line for his lunch and carry a tray to a table. The school lunch staff will be at hand to help children who are new to the school, but it may be helpful to practise these skills in a role-play game with your child. You may want to try giving him a tray for his lunch at home, and encouraging him to carry it to the table himself if you know he will have to do this at school.

Behaviour

Children of this age are often still learning to curb their tempers and to follow rules. If you have established firm boundaries from an early age, it will be far easier for your child to understand the rules he is obliged to follow at school and to behave well. If, however, your child has learnt that you will always give in if he makes enough fuss, it may be far more difficult for him to do as he is told at school.

Explain to your child that the teacher is in charge of all the children in the class, and that it is important to listen to what he or she says. You may want to try to practise by setting some basic rules at home that your child needs to follow, or by getting him to follow some simple instructions. Encouraging him to tidy up his toys after playtime is a good way to start to establish the type of discipline he will need to be able to follow at school, and you can make a game of this by singing as you tidy or by getting him to count his toys.

Concentration

A lot of the learning that takes place in the early years at school is play-based, but children will spend some time sitting still and listening or focusing on one activity. If your child has spent time in a nursery or playgroup in the past, he will have some experience of story time or circle time and will know how to sit still and concentrate, but for those who haven't ever done this before it can be more difficult. Very lively children can find it quite a challenge to have to sit still at this age, and you may want to try to encourage some quiet, focused activities, such as puzzles or games, at home to help with this. Don't expect too much at first but aim to gradually build up the amount of time you spend sitting quietly together doing an activity. Concentration is a skill that can take time to develop for some children, but the more that you are able to spend focused time at home together, the easier it will be for your child to establish this at school.

Social skills

Sharing and taking turns do not come naturally to children and they have to learn these skills. Children who have been to nurseries or playgroups often have more advanced social skills as they've had more practice at negotiating with others of the same age, but learning still tends to be an ongoing process. Parents sometimes have a false impression of their own children if they only see them in adult company as adults tend to ask for things politely and to encourage sharing in a positive way, but of course children deal with things very differently when they are left to their own devices.

If your child doesn't usually spend much time with children of his age, try to take him to play sessions at a local soft play area or playground, or join a music, sport or dance class so that he will have the opportunity to interact with other children.

If you are able to get to know other parents from your child's class in advance, this is a good opportunity to arrange playdates or outings that can help to build confidence for the first few weeks of school. Don't forget that children learn from their parents, and if you are outgoing and sociable it is far more likely that your child will follow suit. If you tend to avoid social situations wherever you can, your child will not have such a clear role model for socialising and may be less confident about mixing with others.

Language

Children develop at their own pace when it comes to language skills, but you can help your child by talking to him and reading stories. These things may be very simple and parents can sometimes overlook them in the urge to ensure that children can count and recognise letters and so on, but they are key to your child's development.

When you are busy, it can be surprisingly hard to find space to just sit and talk to a child, but it is essential to make time to chat with him as this will help to develop his vocabulary and wider language skills. Listening to what he has to say, asking questions and encouraging him to listen, too, will all contribute to his development. It is also important to continue with the routine of reading your child a story before he goes to bed and to read at other times of the day, too, if you can.

Reading skills

Some children are keen to learn to read very early, and will enjoy looking at letters and starting to make sounds. Others may seem less keen, and parents do sometimes worry that their child doesn't seem to be interested. Try to remember that you can do a lot to help your child in an enjoyable, informal way and that this is just as important.

Reading to your child is a crucial first step. The more you read together, the more your child will become aware of books and this will help him understand the concept of reading. It will also help his vocabulary. When you read, it is helpful to discuss the story and pictures with your child as this will develop his reading comprehension. Once you have finished a book, you can ask your child what the story was about or discuss key points in the narrative. If you point at the words as you are reading, your child will start to make the connection between the printed words and the story, and will be able to watch how you read them. Always let your child hold the book if he wants to, and encourage him to 'read' books to you if he is keen to do so. Joining your local library will allow your child to choose new books for himself on a regular basis.

One good way to encourage your child to learn is to incorporate letters and sounds into your daily routine, rather than sitting a child down with an alphabet book and attempting to teach the sounds that letters make. You can buy, online or from toy shops, games aimed specifically at young children that help to teach letters and sounds. The more that learning seems to be fun and the more play-based the activity is, the more likely it is that your child will want to participate. Rhyming games are important, too, and children often really enjoy these.

Parents often try to teach young children to recognise the alphabet using capital letters, but in fact most of the letters we use are lower case and it is better to focus on lower-case letters if you are trying to help prepare your child for school.

Don't worry if your child doesn't seem particularly interested in learning letters. Keep reading to him, keep playing rhyming games and pointing out the sounds that letters make. If you try to force him to sit down and learn, you will be planting seeds of negativity about learning and it is far better to wait until he is ready. Children who start learning to read later often make much faster progress, so it doesn't always follow that those who learn first will continue to be further ahead. Often the key to reading is finding the right books – children will be more motivated to work out what the words say when they are interested in the subject matter, for example, dinosaurs or fairies.

Don't forget that one of the things that will encourage a child to read is a sense that learning is fun. If your child sees you reading and knows that this is an activity you enjoy, it will help make it more appealing to him, too!

Writing skills

Your child will probably be able to recognise his name by the time he starts school and, if he hasn't already, it's a good idea to get him to try to copy his name. In order to be able to write, your child will have to feel confident holding a pencil and this is a skill he can learn through drawing, which is why it is so important to encourage your child's creativity! Colouring in, tracing and painting will all help develop pencil control and will make your child more aware of how to create the shapes he will need to learn when it comes to writing. Your child's fine motor skills, which are key here, will also be developed by other games, such as playing with building blocks, jigsaws and craft activities involving cutting things out and sticking.

By the time your child joins the reception class, he is likely to be showing a preference for using one hand rather than the other for drawing and painting. Most children initially use both hands, and you should allow the preference to develop naturally rather than trying to force your child to use one hand rather than the other. However, by the time children are beginning to write they have normally established this. If you, or your partner, are left-handed there is a higher chance that your child will be left-handed, too.

Your child will probably have had some practice at writing his own name if nothing else before he starts school, and you can encourage him to keep doing this by asking him to add his name to his pictures or paintings. However, when it comes to learning to write more formally, having fun with finger painting, cutting and glueing, sticking and stencils can be just as helpful in establishing the skills needed at this stage.

Numeracy

As with reading, the way to encourage a young child to develop an interest in numbers is to make it fun. Children often enjoy counting games, making patterns and weighing and measuring, all of which can help their numeracy skills. It is surprisingly easy to incorporate number games into your day-to-day activities. Baking or cooking together is an excellent way to teach a child about weighing and measuring. You can also discuss time when you use the oven, and encourage your child to help you to work out when the food will be ready. There are lots of opportunities for practising numeracy skills at the shops or supermarket. Your child can look at prices and work out how much things will cost, you can encourage simple addition by adding up how many items you need and relative values by working out which product is most expensive. You may be able to get your child to weigh fruit and vegetables at the supermarket. You can even integrate numeracy skills into a trip to the park – encourage your child to count the number of ducks on the pond, or children in the playground! This will not only help your child to understand the basic concepts of numeracy, but will also let him see that numeracy skills are an important part of daily life and not something that only happens at school.

Recognising shapes and patterns and an understanding of relative sizes are all skills that can be encouraged through play – matching, comparing and counting games are useful, as are blocks, bricks and Lego, which can help children to grasp concepts such as bigger or smaller and higher or lower. Time is another key area, and you can help your child to develop an understanding of time by talking to him about his daily routine and what time it is when he has breakfast or finishes school or goes to bed. You can also discuss how long is spent on different activities, such as cleaning his teeth, or eating his supper. Looking forward to events in the future, such as his birthday, and discussing what he did last weekend or at nursery the day before, will all help him to clarify his understanding of the passage of time.

Learning through play

We have seen how important it is to make learning fun for small children, and the same applies to many of the practical skills that your child will need during his time at primary school. You may not always be aware of quite how important the games that you play with your child can be, for example:

- Building and stacking bricks, rolling a ball and catching and throwing will all improve hand–eye co-ordination.

- Jigsaws, dot-to-dot puzzles, games identifying colour and shape, such as matching the socks from your laundry basket, will all help improve perception and visual skills.

- Playing dominos, matching games and Simon Says will help your child's memory.

- Dressing up, role-play and make-believe games will help his imagination.

- Listening to story tapes or rhymes will help with listening skills.

- Playing Follow the Leader, charades and team games can help develop social skills.

- Cutting, colouring, drawing and craft activities will improve fine motor skills (actions that develop the use of smaller muscles).

- Dancing, swimming, swinging, sliding and riding trikes and scooters will develop gross motor skills (actions that develop the use of bigger muscles).

- Just talking and reading will have an impact on your child's vocabulary and language.

The Last Few Weeks

During the weeks leading up to the time that your child starts school, make sure you keep reinforcing your positive messages about the experience. Listen to any concerns he may have and try to reassure him. If he doesn't want to talk about school, don't keep bringing the subject up – his reluctance to talk may be his way of dealing with the impending change. Try not to let any emotions you may be feeling become obvious to him. Finally, make sure he gets lots of sleep and eats well. Starting school is going to be a big step in his life and he will need all the energy he can muster!

Case History:
Hannah and Mia – Preparing for School

We started thinking about schools when we moved into the area, and then we began looking a year before the girls were due to start. We knew we weren't going to have that much choice because both the schools close to us are very oversubscribed. Our nearest school is a church school, and we really wanted the girls to go there, not because we are religious but because it is small and friendly and we couldn't imagine a better start for the girls. We had a real risk that we wouldn't get into either school, though, and that was the worry.

We could apply for three schools, so we put the faith school first, and I didn't realise quite how anxious I was until about a week before. Then the night before the letters were due to arrive, they published the admissions criteria on the local authority website. The catchment area for our first choice went to 0.198 miles and we were up looking at mapping software websites trying to work out if we were that close. We thought we might be just inside the catchment but we weren't certain. It was so stressful.

I was working at home the next day, and the moment I heard the letterbox I went running to get the letter – I'm sure the postman must have heard my happy squeal from outside. We were just so pleased. It's our nearest school and it is small and friendly. It reminded me of my primary school and just felt really nice. It was also one of the only schools in the area with a single intake, which meant we didn't have the dilemma of having to decide whether to separate the girls. I know some schools will go against parents' wishes to separate twins, and I think our two are independent enough that they don't need artificially separating from one another – I didn't want them to have that worry.

As the date for starting school got closer, Hannah was really up for it but Mia was a lot more fragile about it. We only really realised what was going on when we went out to buy their school shoes about three weeks before term started. We went out for lunch afterwards, and Mia was just really quiet and withdrawn. My husband asked her if she was worried about starting school and she just burst into tears and threw herself at him. We realised that every time we talked about it she was going quiet. I think it was the worry of leaving nursery and her friends rather than the fear of starting school, but the two things were intertwined. Eventually she said she was worried that Hannah would find a new friend at school and wouldn't want to be her friend any more, which was just heartbreaking. Hannah is the class clown and is always everybody's best friend, but Mia tends to have a couple of friends and that's it.

In terms of preparation, we didn't do anything specific academically. The girls were born in September, so they are on the older side of their year, and they were getting bored at their day nursery so we have done some basic phonics and counting with them. They can spell a few basic words, but we didn't do it especially for school. The things we did do in preparation for school were more social, like eating properly with a knife and fork, learning how to wipe their bottom and how to do up zips and buttons.

At the end of the term before they started school, the staff did a session for new parents and they went through the things they like the kids to be able to do before school. They gave us a list so that we could do it over the summer. It was things like learning to dress themselves and go to the toilet alone. A lot of it was common sense, but it does stop you worrying about what you might have missed. The school did stress at the meeting that it was the lifestyle things that are important not the educational ones – it doesn't matter if a child can't count because that is what they are going to school to learn. They also gave us a list of books about starting school in case the children were anxious.

One thing that I really like is the buddy system they run at the school. All the children in reception are assigned a Year Five child to 'adopt' them. The buddy meets them on the first day and then checks that they are okay at playtime and at lunchtime. Their buddies are lovely and the girls worship them. It has made such a difference to them settling in.

The thing I've found weird about the transition from nursery to school is not knowing everything they're doing. At nursery we could wander in and chat about what they'd been doing with their key worker, get a list of exactly what they'd eaten and what they'd done all day. Now, I have to rely on what they tell me and I did feel a bit lost at first. It is a big change.

4

The First Days
and Weeks at School

When your child first starts school it is the beginning of a new phase for you as a family. School will become a large part of your child's life, and this will change your daily routines, too. It is a time of transition for a child, as this marks the start of his formal education and also of a new independence. You will want to do all you can to make this run smoothly for him and to prepare both yourself and your child for what lies ahead.

It is important to keep in mind how radical a change starting school can be to a young child. Even small schools can seem daunting, and the older pupils may seem very grown up and rather frightening. Children are often not used to such a long day apart from a parent or carer, or to having their lunch at school. They may find it difficult to have to sit still at first, or to understand when they need to stop talking. The structure of their day, with specific times for play and certain activities, will be new to them. They may not know anyone at their school and even if they do find some familiar faces from playgroups or the local area, they will have to make new friends and learn how to deal with new people. Your child will need to become more independent, doing things for himself without your help, and making his own choices and decisions. Having to take on so many new challenges at such a young age can be difficult at first and it is not surprising that it can take children a while to settle into school.

Although teething problems are common, most children enjoy primary school once they are settled. Parents can do a lot to make the transition easier, by offering practical and emotional support and by preparing their children as best they can for what lies ahead.

The Day Before Your Child Starts School

If you have spent some time preparing your child for school, you will probably have thought about most of the issues that may arise beforehand. There may still be some last-minute preparations the day before your child starts school to ensure he is as ready as he can be:

- If your child is going to be wearing uniform, make sure everything is clean and ready to wear. If the school doesn't have a uniform, you may want to ask your child whether there's anything specific that he'd like to wear for school, but make sure it is something practical and not a special item of clothing that he is going to worry about getting dirty. Don't forget to do a last-minute label check to ensure everything is clearly marked with your child's name.

- If your child is having packed lunch, you may want to take him shopping with you to choose some food that he would like for lunch. Do check beforehand whether there are any school rules about packed lunches; some schools have healthy eating policies and may not allow foods such as sweets or crisps and fizzy or sugary drinks in children's packed lunches. The school welcome pack or introductory literature should have mentioned any rules about packed lunches, but it may be worth checking if you are planning to give him something that you aren't sure about. Make sure your child is going to be able to open any bottles, cartons or tubs that you give him at lunchtime as it can be very upsetting for a child to be faced with something he can't get open on his first day. You may also want to think twice before adding anything very strong-smelling or unusual, particularly if your child is prone to being sensitive, as other children may remark on things like this. Although you don't want to be limited in your choices of food for your own child by what other children find acceptable, it can help for the first few weeks at least if you don't provide anything too unusual that might stand out.

- If your child has any medical conditions or allergies, make sure that the school is informed and that you have briefed them on any medicines that may need to be administered. Most schools are now used to dealing with children with asthma and other common allergies, and many are now nut-free zones where parents are informed not to add any nut products to children's lunchboxes, but it is still essential that the school is informed and that they are aware what action to take (for example, if your child may need his asthma pump for asthma or an EpiPen for an allergy).

- If your child needs to take a school bag with a pencil case or a PE kit, make sure you have this ready the night before.

- Remind your child of any friends who will be at school when he arrives there in the morning. It will help him approach the new day with confidence if he knows there will be some familiar faces.

- Make sure your child has a good evening meal. Cook something you know he enjoys as he will need lots of energy for his first day.

- Try to get him to go to bed early. He may be excited and find it hard to sleep, so if he goes to bed a little earlier than usual this may help.

- If he has any last-minute concerns or worries, do listen to him even if you feel they aren't things that really matter. Some children will be quite anxious, however much preparation you have done and reassurance you have given. Make a point of taking your child seriously, acknowledging his fears and responding to any problems as best you can. Try to focus on the positives, and boost his confidence by spending time with him and giving him lots of hugs. Keep things as calm as you can – you may want to take the focus away from school by talking about what you might do the next evening or at the weekend to reassure him that life is not going to be turned completely upside down just because he is starting school.

● Tell him what a great day he will have tomorrow!

Before School on the First Day

You will want to do all you can to make the morning of your child's first day at school run smoothly and calmly so that your child arrives at school in the best possible frame of mind.

● Set your own alarm early so that you are up in plenty of time and not rushing around. If you are calm and have everything prepared, this will help your child feel calmer.

● Get your child up in plenty of time, too, so that he doesn't feel rushed and can get dressed and eat breakfast at his own pace.

● Give your child a good breakfast before he goes to school. If he will eat porridge or a cooked breakfast, this will help set him up for the day, but if he's not a big breakfast eater, do ensure that he has at least something before he sets off for school.

● Make sure your child has something to drink with his breakfast, too. Having a drink is just as important as eating as children can sometimes forget to drink during the day when they are busy, and dehydration can make them tired and irritable.

- Check that your child has everything he needs before you leave the house.

- Leave the house in plenty of time, especially if you are driving as you don't want to get stressed if you run into traffic.

Arriving at School

Many schools have some kind of settling-in procedure to help the transition into primary school. Your child may begin by attending for just half the day on his first day, or even throughout his first week. Some schools stagger the entrance dates slightly, so that the teacher isn't faced with 30 new children all starting at the same time and can focus on helping a handful of new children to settle in each day.

- You may be able to stay with your child for a little while on the first day. Staff will have made you aware of what is expected, and you should be guided by them in this. They know that children may feel more confident if a parent is allowed to stay for a while, and if you know that your child is feeling particularly anxious, you will want to let the staff know.

- Be mindful that it is often the parent who is more worried and emotional than their child and it is not unusual to find that the parents are the ones shedding tears at the gate rather than their children. If you are feeling anxious, try not to transmit this to your child.

- Before you leave, make sure your child knows who will be collecting him and when, otherwise he may worry about this during the day.

- The school should have all your contact details, but if you have any concerns, you can always check with the school office that they have the correct ones. You may also want to find out if there is a number that you can call during the day to check that your child has settled in.

- Once you are ready to go, tell your child that you are leaving and when you will be back. Try to be fairly brief and to the point – a long, lingering farewell may be what you want at this stage, but it can make it more difficult for your child.

- When you leave the classroom, don't stay outside looking through the windows but make sure you go right away. Even if your child is settled and happy in the classroom, it may be unsettling for him if he suddenly notices you outside.

- If your child is upset when you go, try to remember that this is not likely to last for long. Talk to the teacher if your child doesn't seem to want to let you go, and remember that most teachers will have seen this before and will have some strategies to help deal with it. Your child will usually be encouraged to do something he finds interesting in order to minimise any separation anxiety.

How you feel

Parents are sometimes surprised by how emotional they feel about their child's first day at school. You know, more than he does, that this is the start of a new phase of your lives. He will become more independent and will start to have a world of his own, where he makes his own decisions and has his own friends. This transition is a big change for the entire family. It is perfectly normal to feel upset about this, and to worry about how your child will cope with things; up until now, you may have felt in control of your child's life and able to protect him from problems. Even at nursery, you may have had more say as a parent about how things are done, and had more involvement, but now your child will be in a larger class at school, looked after by someone you may not know at all, and he will have to learn how to cope by himself.

The school day can seem very long, and you may worry about whether he will eat lunch, remember to go to the toilet or be able to do up his coat. If you have been a stay-at-home mum, especially if you don't have any younger children at home, your feelings may be exacerbated by questions about your own role and how you use your time during school hours. For working mothers, there is sometimes a feeling of worry and guilt if you are not able to be there to pick your child up at the end of the school day and he has to go on to an after-school club or carer. This first step towards independence can seem hugely significant, and may stir up all kinds of emotions, which sometimes comes as a surprise. Learning to let go isn't easy, but your child will gradually reap the benefits of this newfound independence even if there are some hiccups along the way.

Many parents find that it helps if they get involved in school life, so that they are able to have more of an insight into their child's new world. Joining the Parents' Association or Friends of the School or volunteering to help with reading or accompanying the children on trips can enable you to feel a part of the school. If you do feel tearful on the first day, make sure your child doesn't see you looking upset as he may feel that you know something he doesn't and that he ought to be worried.

After School on the First Day

The first day at school will have been full of exciting new things for your child, and he will have had a lot to absorb and learn. Bear in mind that most children are completely exhausted after their first day.

- Make sure you get to school early, ready to greet your child as soon as he comes out or you may be allowed in to pick him up (if you work full-time, consider taking some annual leave around this time). He will be looking out for you and will be worried if you are late. If you can arrive a little early for at least the first few weeks of school, this will be helpful as children do find it upsetting if they are always the last one to be picked up.

- Try not to have any after-school activities for at least the first week. It's probably a good idea to cut after-school activities back to a minimum during his first term as these early weeks and months at school are very tiring for a young child and he will want to focus on what goes on during the day.

- Take a healthy snack with you for your child to eat when you pick him up from school, preferably something you know he really likes, and a drink. He is likely to be very hungry and thirsty by the end of the school day.

- Of course, you will want to know about every moment of your child's day, but try to understand that he may not feel ready to talk about it. Don't bombard him with questions if he seems tired as this is more likely to make him clam up altogether. Some children will be keen to tell you about everything that has happened, but others may simply be too tired to launch into a detailed explanation about all that has happened during the day.

- If you ask questions, try to make them specific – for example 'What did you have for lunch?', 'Who did you play with?' – rather than vague questions about whether he's enjoyed his day; he may find it hard to answer this type of question.

- Cook something you know he likes for supper and encourage him to eat well. He will need all his energy for the rest of his week.

- Don't try to make him do anything educational in the evening. If he wants to relax and watch TV for a while, that's fine. He has had a busy day filled with new activities and you need to give him some breathing space.

● An early night is a good idea!

The First Week

Your child will take some time to adjust to his new routine, and you will still be adjusting, too. Don't forget what a big change this is in his life, and that you may need to be patient with him during the first week or two.

● Children can become very grumpy when they first start at school and parents often worry that this must be a sign that they are unhappy, that they are having problems at school or that they aren't settling down. In fact, sometimes it is simple exhaustion. It's easy to underestimate what a big change this is in a small child's life – to be in a school with much older children, to be in a large class with a new teacher and new friends, to have to absorb huge amounts of new information every day. It is hardly surprising that children get tired or that they act differently at home. Your child may have been on his best behaviour all day and once he's back with his family, he may feel that at last he can let go. If he seems angry and bad-tempered, try to be as patient with him as you can.

● Try to give your child as much attention as you can after school. Listen to him if he wants to talk, and make sure you show an interest in everything he says about his day at school.

- Keep things at home as stable as you can and continue with your familiar routines so that he can see that the rest of your family life can go on as normal despite starting at school.

- You can always ask your child's teacher or classroom assistant how he is getting on and whether there have been any issues that you should be aware of. Equally, if there's anything that you are worried about, don't feel afraid to ask or to check up on things. Teachers will be used to parents having some concerns during the first few weeks.

- If you're a stay-at-home mum and have been used to having your child around for most of the day, you may find that your days feel rather empty or lonely for the first few weeks even if you have a younger child to care for. Try to keep busy and to arrange things to do so that you don't miss your older child too much during the day.

Common Problems in the First Term

Schools tend to be busy, noisy and crowded, and it can be hard for your child to know quite where he fits in. Be aware of any changes in your child's behaviour that may indicate that he isn't settling, for example if he seems very withdrawn or unhappy. However, remember that it's normal to have some teething problems, and even children who take a little while to feel comfortable at school will usually find that any early issues are soon forgotten. It can help if your child feels that you are interested and involved with his new life, and going along to any school events such as fairs or concerts will help to achieve this.

Problems making friends

Some children are more outgoing than others and may make friends easily. Others do find it more difficult and may be rather overwhelmed by the large numbers of children in the playground at playtime.

If your child tells you that he is finding playtimes difficult, do not immediately assume the worst. Sometimes children say things that sound heartbreaking to a loving parent; for example, 'No one likes me at school', 'I don't have anyone to play with at playtime' or 'I don't have any friends'. Of course, you would want to listen carefully and take this seriously, but you may find if you ask more questions that what this really means is that your child was alone at playtime for a few minutes in between games rather than he spent the entire break sitting by himself. If you are at all worried, do speak to his teacher. The playground staff will be able to make sure that he isn't always alone or isolated at break time, and the teacher may be able to encourage others to play games that all the children can join in with.

Many primary schools have mentoring or buddy schemes with older children taking the role of Prefects or Young Leaders, who involve younger children in games and activities at playtime. These schemes can be very successful as older children often enjoy taking the responsibility for ensuring that all the younger children are involved and that they don't feel lonely or isolated at breaks, while the younger children enjoy having much older 'friends' who will play with them during breaks. If you think your child may be having problems at playtimes, you can always ask whether the school operates any such scheme.

Don't forget that not all children want to be the centre of attention, and if your child says he plays by himself but doesn't seem upset by this, he may be perfectly happy. Sometimes your child may not want to join in with boisterous games and may want to get on with his own activities. It is only if your child is having problems developing his social skills, is anxious or upset, or is being deliberately excluded by other children that you would want to intervene.

Children sometimes come home with reports of disputes or problems that have occurred with other children at school, and it can be tempting for parents to wade in and try to sort things out. You should always be careful about getting involved in issues your child may have with friends at school and try to remember that you are being given a one-sided view of the situation. It is easy to assume that your child is in the right and is being treated unfairly or even unkindly, but sometimes the other child or children involved will feel just the same way about the situation. It is better to listen to your child carefully and then make some positive suggestions, such as playing with another friend or trying to negotiate.

Children of this age can sometimes be unkind to one another, and if you have any serious concerns of course it is always worth having a quiet word with the class teacher. Try not to jump to conclusions about other children's behaviour or contact other parents and making accusations. Learning to deal with other people is an important skill that children need to master, and if you keep intervening every time your child has an issue with another child, you will make it far more difficult for him in the future. Children can often work out how to deal with problems themselves if you encourage them to do so.

Bullying

Although bullying is unlikely at this age, all schools are aware that bullying can be a serious problem for young children, and will have strategies in place to deal with it. Bullying isn't just about physical violence such as hitting or pushing, it can also be verbal, where a child is teased unkindly or called names. Sometimes it can even be psychological, where rumours are spread about a child or he is deliberately excluded.

Bullying can happen to boys and girls, but in primary schools it is apparently more common among girls as they tend to form tight-knit friendship groups and are more likely to leave others out. If your child comes home upset and tells you that other children have been deliberately unkind, it can be hard to react calmly. Remember that sometimes this will be one incident that has felt highly significant to your child, but may be forgotten by the next day.

If you feel a pattern is developing and you suspect that your child is being bullied, the most important thing is to encourage your child to talk about it and to let him know that you are there to support him. There are some signs that can indicate that a child may be being bullied and they include:

1. Being withdrawn or anxious.

2. Challenging behaviour at home.

3. Not wanting to go to school.

4. Feeling 'ill' with tummy aches, headaches or nausea when it's time to go to school.

5. Regression, such as bedwetting or soiling.

6. Having disrupted sleep patterns.

7. Having nightmares.

8. Tearfulness after school.

9. Mood changes.

10. Being disruptive or angry.

11. Saying he hates school.

12. Coming home with damaged clothing or other items.

13. Unexplained bruises or scrapes.

It is important not to jump to conclusions, as some of these signs can just as easily indicate tiredness and may be related to the huge changes your child is experiencing during the first few weeks of school. If you begin to notice a pattern emerging and feel that bullying is a possibility, try to encourage your child to talk about school, friendships, how he gets on with the other children and whether there is anything that is upsetting him.

If your child finds it too upsetting to talk about, don't force him to open up but keep reassuring him that it is not his fault that this has happened and that the problem lies with the other child, or children. Children are sometimes afraid to tell adults or to talk to teachers in case this just makes the problem worse, so it is important to make it clear to your child that he will not get into trouble for talking about what has happened. Do raise the issue with your child's class teacher as soon as you can, and explain what your child has told you. You should ask how the school will deal with the issue and make sure you are happy with this – you may also want to ask to see the school bullying policy.

It is important, however, to keep in mind at this stage that disagreements between children and even some unkindness does not necessarily equate to bullying. Parents can jump to the conclusion that a child is being bullied if they come home talking about something that they have felt was wrong or unfair. Of course you should listen sympathetically, but remember that children of this age are still learning their social skills and that they can sometimes be unkind or thoughtless without meaning any real harm. Your child needs to learn to deal with this kind of social difficulty and being able to handle it himself is an important part of growing up. Of course, if your child is struggling, you will want to help but try not to cast him in the role of the victim immediately as this may not be in his best interests.

If your child is being bullied, or is having problems with one or more other children, there are some strategies that you can use to help him through this:

- Make sure that your child understands that the bullying isn't his fault and that it is unacceptable behaviour.

- Keep praising him and try to do all that you can to boost his self-confidence as this will make him less vulnerable.

- Try to help him deal with the incidents at school by talking about how to handle them. Encourage him to walk away from a situation where he is being bullied and to understand that this is a good way of dealing with it.

- Always leave time to listen to your child's problems.

- Explain to your child that people who are happy don't need to bully others. Bullies are usually jealous, insecure or angry inside and they are not people who are confident or contented.

Schools are often very good at dealing with bullying quickly and effectively, but they have to know about it to be able to do this. Once you have spoken to your child's teacher, do keep in touch with the school until you are satisfied that the problem has been dealt with effectively.

Discovering that your child has been bullying another child can be just as shocking and upsetting for a parent, as no one wants to think that their own offspring could be capable of this kind of behaviour. Children who bully others may do so for a variety of reasons, and it can even be as a result of having been bullied first themselves. Bullying behaviour can sometimes alert parents to the fact that a child is feeling overlooked, and it may be linked to other events in your child's life which have perhaps made him feel insecure. Sometimes what happens at home can have an influence here, as children who have experienced a more aggressive or hostile atmosphere or those who are punished harshly are more likely to be aggressive to other children. Children who bully others may have always been encouraged to fight back and it is important to ensure that your child understands the difference between being assertive and being aggressive. It can also be the result of copying the behaviour of another child or an adult. Sometimes, however, there is no clear reason why a child has been unkind to others, but it is still behaviour that you will want to curb as soon as you can.

It is not nice to think of your child as a bully, and parents are sometimes reluctant to accept that what their child has done is wrong, feeling that he must have been treated unfairly or that he was provoked into behaving badly. It is true that sometimes the label can be used unfairly, but it is important to try to look at the situation as objectively as you can rather than immediately assuming that your child would never act in this way. Even well-behaved children can occasionally get swept up into being unkind or aggressive. Ensuring that your child doesn't act in this way again, even if he does feel someone else is provoking him, is vital. If your child gets a reputation for being a bully it can be a hard label to lose, and it is more difficult to turn things around when others expect him to respond in an aggressive way.

If you discover that your child has been bullying others, there are some steps you can take that may help:

- Begin by talking to your child about what has happened, and trying to get to the bottom of why he acted in the way he did.

- Don't forget that in this situation your child may well try to make himself out to be the innocent party, and you need to make it clear that although you are willing to listen carefully and empathetically to his side of the story, you are not going to allow him to be unaccountable for unkind or hurtful behaviour.

- Make it clear that the way your child has behaved is unacceptable, but stress that it is the behaviour you are unhappy with rather than your child himself. Explain that it is not too late to remedy matters.

- Try to encourage him to put himself into the other child's shoes for a change and ask him how he would feel if someone said, or did, these things to him.

- He should be encouraged to apologise, but you may want to discuss whether there is anything else he could do that would make the other child, or children, feel less upset about what has happened.

- Think about your child's exposure to violence on TV or through computer games. If he does play games or see programmes that are not suitable for his age, putting a stop to this may help.

- It is also worth thinking about the way you react in your home when you are angry. If you, or other members of the family, have a tendency to fly off the handle, or to lash out either verbally or physically, curbing your own behaviour may have a positive effect.

- Make sure that you reward your child whenever he shows kindness or empathy to others and praise him for this.

- If you take action quickly and make it clear that this behaviour is unacceptable and won't be tolerated, you have a good chance of remedying the situation effectively.

Homework

Most schools will give very little in the way of homework when children first start school, but they may encourage you to read every day with your child or to spend a little time practising letters or numbers.

Some children are keen to show what they've learnt and may want to do any suggested homework right away, but don't worry if your child isn't keen. You may find that you can incorporate school reading into your bedtime routine if you usually read your child a bedtime story, and this can be an easy way to avoid making an issue of homework.

If your child is really resistant to doing any schoolwork at home, don't force him to sit down and do it. It's far better to talk to his teacher and explain how he's reacting. Sometimes the teacher may have some tips to make the learning fun so that it doesn't seem like more work after a busy day at school. Remember that your child will be very tired during the first few months at school, and may just need to switch off when he gets home.

Change in behaviour

It is surprisingly common for children to behave badly at home when they first start school. They may be grumpy or disobedient, have tantrums or just seem angry and aggressive. Try not to panic if your child seems to have lost the ability to behave well in the first few weeks of school. Be patient and deal with any bad behaviour as calmly as you can, reacting in just the way that you normally would.

It can be worrying for a parent as you may feel that your child has a changed personality and that you have lost your usually happy, cheerful child. Rest assured that bad behaviour usually turns out to be down to tiredness and the enormous life change. You will tend to find that it starts to tail off after a few weeks as your child becomes more accustomed to school life and his new daily routines. If there is no improvement by the end of the first half term, you may want to find out whether there are any issues at school that you haven't been aware of that could be causing difficulties for your child.

Regressive behaviour

Some children react to starting school by showing regressive behaviour at home. They may become very babyish, for example starting thumb-sucking, wanting to be fed at mealtimes or asking to sleep in a cot. Don't forget that your still very young child has had to be 'grown up' all day at school, and may not feel entirely ready for it. Your child may be feeling worried or uncertain, and regressive behaviour can sometimes become an outlet for this.

Try not to be unduly worried, and to calmly encourage your child to act his age without making too much fuss about it. Be positive about all the things your child can enjoy now he is old enough to go to school, but don't make it into a big issue. Children will usually get over this kind of behaviour as they relax into being at school. In most cases, not making too much of it and focusing on rewarding your child for good behaviour rather than worrying about the regressive behaviour will be sufficient to start to see a gradual improvement in your child's behaviour. There are some things you can do which may help:

- Communication is key so make it clear to your child that you want to listen to his worries. Sit down with him and listen properly to what he has to say. Don't dismiss his concerns and do try to suggest some solutions.

- Regression is often associated with feelings of anxiety. Giving your child lots of praise, reassurance and extra cuddles can help to address any underlying feelings of insecurity.

- Make some extra time for your child when he comes home from school, or when you come home from work. Whether you spend this time just chatting to your child, playing a board game together or reading books doesn't matter, but make sure you set aside proper time and don't try to do other tasks simultaneously.

- You can also try to give your child extra time at bedtime, either reading him additional books before bed, spending time helping him with his reading or leaving some space to talk.

It is only if the issues with regression seem to be dragging on and are starting to cause you some concern that you will want to look more closely at how your child is settling into school and whether there are any issues that you may be unaware of that may be making him feel insecure.

Feeling overwhelmed by other children at school

Primary schools can seem like big places to small children, especially if their only experience of being away from their parents has been at a cosy playgroup or nursery. The playground, in particular, can seem like an alarming environment, with lots of bigger children rushing around making lots of noise at playtime. At many schools, the younger children play separately, at least at first, and this can give them some space to adjust.

Do all that you can in advance to prevent this from becoming an issue by making sure your child has some experience of being in busy environments, perhaps at the local shopping centre or swimming pool at the weekend. The more time your child has spent with lots of other people, the less worrying the playground environment will be.

If your child does come home and tell you that he finds the playground a bit much, you may want to encourage him to find one or two particular friends to be with at playtimes. You can also suggest that he stays away from the busier areas of the playground and does something quieter instead – many schools have some quiet areas of the playground. If there are prefects or school leaders, tell him that he can always go to them or to a member of staff if he is feeling upset. It can take a while to adjust to the bustle of school, but parents generally find that even the most sensitive child soon finds his own niche in the playground.

Reluctance to go to school

Parents want their children to be happy at school and to enjoy it, but children can sometimes seem reluctant to go to school or may say that they don't like school and that they want to stay at home. This can happen suddenly after an initially happy start and is naturally worrying for a parent. It may be that something has happened to upset them in the playground or in the classroom and you will want to try to get to the bottom of this by asking gentle questions. Sometimes a small incident or worry can have taken on a great deal of significance for a child, and you may find it relatively easy to reassure him once you understand the problem. Don't hesitate to talk to your child's teacher if you feel it is something he or she ought to be aware of.

Sometimes having started school quite cheerfully, the novelty has finally worn off and your child is realising that he's going to have to go to school every day now. Even if your child quite enjoys school, the reality of having to be up and in school all day five days a week can be a rather daunting prospect. If he has younger siblings who are at home with you or with a carer, he may resent the fact that they are still spending their days going to the park and doing all the things he used to enjoy. Make sure you keep being positive about school and about the things he is doing there to encourage him to feel the same way. Tell him how jealous his younger sibling or siblings are that he gets to go and have fun at school all day, learning lots of new things, while they are stuck at home following the same old routine. Separation anxiety can sometimes be at the root of the problem, as detailed below.

Separation anxiety

Most children go off to school quite happily after a few weeks, even if they have had some tearful days at the beginning. If your child continues to be worried or sad at the moment you leave it isn't necessarily a cause for great concern as long as it isn't affecting him for the rest of the day once you've gone. There are a number of things you can do that may help with this:

- Anxiety can start to build long before you get to the school gate. If your child wakes up and immediately starts worrying about what is going to happen at school, listen to what he has to say and try to answer any specific fears – for example, your child may be worried about not knowing where to go at lunchtime or about whether he can manage to put on his own trainers for PE. It may be that you can allay some of his worries immediately if you spend five minutes discussing his concerns.

- If he is just worried about school in general, trying to get him to focus on other things may help. Sometimes parents can talk too much about school in the early days, making it loom alarmingly large for a young child. Let him choose what he wants for breakfast, and encourage him to help you prepare it or to lay the table. A school day can feel very long and focusing on what you are going to do when you pick him up or when you get home from work, and making sure that it is something he enjoys, can shift his attention to the fact that there is still more of the day to be enjoyed after school.

- During the journey to school you may be able to engage him in a game, such as I Spy or something else he likes so that he doesn't spend the journey worrying. Make sure you leave plenty of time for the journey, as if you are rushed and harassed this is going to make your child feel anxious.

- Don't prolong the moment of separation or sneak off without saying goodbye. It can seem easier to leave when your child is absorbed in an activity but it is important that he knows that you are leaving. It can make it more difficult later on if he wasn't aware that you had gone. It can be helpful to develop a familiar way of saying goodbye to your child, which you can start establishing even before he starts school. It doesn't have to be complicated – perhaps just a special big hug and kiss, or a last wave as you go out – but some kind of regular routine whenever you leave your child can be helpful as he will know what to expect.

- Some experts suggest leaving something of yours with your child during the day so that he has a reminder of you with him if he feels insecure or anxious. This may help in some circumstances, but you would need to be sure that it isn't going to be a constant reminder of the fact that you aren't there as this may make matters worse. It is also important to be sure that there is no danger of whatever it is getting mislaid in a busy classroom or playground as again this could make the situation more difficult.

- Try not to be overprotective as this can feed your child's anxieties. If he does seem upset, reassure him that he will be fine, that you are leaving but that you will be back at the end of the day to collect him. If he sees that you are upset and are being affected by tearful partings, this may exacerbate the problem.

Obviously, leaving a child who seems distressed is always very upsetting, and sometimes it can be difficult to tell whether your child just finds saying goodbye difficult or whether he has a more serious problem. Remember that it is extremely common for children to experience some separation anxiety when they start school and to have some difficulties settling. This can often continue for the first few weeks, or even months, without being an indication of a more serious underlying problem. It is really only when there is no improvement in the anxiety or when you can sense that your child is still very unhappy about school that this may indicate an issue that needs addressing. There are some signs that may indicate that your child is finding it particularly tough:

1. He may regularly complain of being ill with tummy aches or headaches when he has to go to school or when you leave him there. Many children will do this now and again, but if it is happening on a regular basis, it would suggest that something is amiss.

2. He may cling to you to try to stop you leaving, or have tantrums.

3. He may start refusing to go to school at all.

4. He may have nightmares or find it difficult to get to sleep because he is worried.

5. He may become very frightened or worried about other things and start to withdraw from family life.

If you feel that your child has a more serious issue, do talk to the class teacher, who may be able to reassure you or suggest some ways to help. There are a number of strategies that may be beneficial for a child who is experiencing separation anxiety:

- It can be useful to identify a member of staff or a place in the school that he can go to if he is feeling at all anxious during the day.

- Don't dismiss your child's feelings. Encourage him to talk and listen carefully to what he has to say, while offering reassurance.

- Sometimes separation anxiety is triggered by worries about whether a parent will be all right when they are away from the child all day, and whether they will be there at the end of the day. Reassure your child that you will spend your day at work or at home, and that you will always be there promptly waiting for him at the end of the school day or when you get back from work. If a child has any degree of separation anxiety, ensuring that you – or whoever else is picking him up – is never late at the end of the school day is essential. Setting a precedent of always arriving 10 minutes early is a good idea.

- Give your child lots of praise when you collect him from school. Show that you are interested in what he has been doing and impressed by his work, so that he can feel positive about his achievements.

- If the situation is deemed to merit intervention, the school may suggest that your child attends for a slightly shorter day or for half-days for a while to help him feel more confident.

- He may be allowed to start the school day a little later, or leave slightly earlier, to help him feel more secure.

- Sometimes counselling sessions may help a child who is suffering severe separation anxiety. This can be very helpful and offering counselling at school to help children through particular difficulties is increasingly common.

Throughout your child's time at school, there will be new challenges and new experiences. Getting your child off to a good start will help him rise to meet these with enthusiasm and confidence. School isn't always easy for children, but learning to deal with problems that he faces along the way is part of growing up and an important learning process. You can make all the difference by supporting your child and by ensuring that he is ready for what lies ahead.

Case History: Freddie – Starting School

Freddie had been at the nursery at the school he was going to, so he already knew it when he started. There was a big group going up from his nursery class, and he knew lots of older kids around the school. The nursery is a separate building but still inside the school grounds, and he'd spent a lot of time going into the 'big school' for assemblies and school fairs. He was looking forward to going up to reception and it didn't cross our minds that he might have a problem settling in.

I was the one who cried when I left him on the first day. He looked so small and serious going into the classroom in his school sweatshirt with his book bag. There were a few of us mums looking tearful as we left the children, but we were careful not to let them see how upset we were. I'm a full-time mum, and it was a big change in my life being at home with just the baby for company. I missed Freddie a lot.

He was very tired for the first few days, but I'd expected that. I was asking him questions about what he'd done and who he'd played with and whether he liked it and what he'd had for lunch. He didn't seem to want to talk about it at all. Whenever he said anything about school it wasn't about the class or the teacher, it was always about the playground and big boys pushing people and running about.

He'd always been a happy kind of kid, but by the end of the week he was horrible. All the way home from school he was kicking the walls of houses and lamp posts and he just refused to talk to me at all. He had a tantrum at bedtime, and I was worried that something was wrong.

He seemed a bit better at the weekend, a lot calmer although he was still quiet, but by the time I got him from school on Monday it was just the same; refusing to talk to me, scuffing his shoes along the pavement, flying off the handle at the least thing. We were wondering whether someone was bullying him, but every time we tried to ask him questions he got so angry. He'd calm down by bedtime, but he didn't want to talk about school at all. I wondered whether he was too young for school, whether we'd chosen the right place, whether there was something wrong with him. I was thinking that maybe I should go to see his class teacher, but I didn't know what to say as it wasn't as if anything had happened.

It was about halfway through the third week that he suddenly started chatting about a book his teacher was reading them in class and how it had made them all laugh. It was nice to know there were some good times in his day. That evening he had quite a long chat with his dad about the puddings you got with your school dinner. From then on, it seemed that every day got a bit better and he was telling us more things about school and being less angry. Looking back, I think it was all down to the change in environment. Starting school is such a huge leap, and he was so tired and overwhelmed that it was coming out as anger and aggression.

5

Dealing with Specific Concerns

If you know, or suspect, that your child has a specific problem that may make school more difficult, you will want to be certain that you have taken this into consideration in your choice of primary school. Some schools are better than others at offering support to children with specific learning difficulties or disabilities. For example, you may feel that a very shy child would be better off in a smaller school, or that a child who is gifted and talented may be more suited to a high-achieving school, where there would be other very bright children.

Some children may have problems that only start to appear at school; for example dyscalculia (see page 168) or dyslexia (see page 164). It can take a while to realise that your child isn't performing as well as you think he should be and to identify the problem. Whatever the nature of your child's specific difficulty, you can help by understanding what is wrong and by doing all you can to support him and to ensure that he doesn't feel undervalued because he has a problem. See page 203 for a list of organisations that offer help, support and information for different conditions.

Shy or Unconfident Children

Many young children are shy or lack self-confidence. This doesn't necessarily have to be a problem, as most will tend to grow out of it with time. Parents may want their children to be confident and to be able to deal with a variety of social situations happily, but it can take time for children to feel at ease. If you are shy or lack confidence yourself, you are far more likely to have a child who has similar traits – children learn social confidence by example. This can be difficult for you as a parent if you have always suffered with shyness or a lack of confidence, and struggled to overcome these traits.

If you feel your child's shyness or lack of confidence is affecting him at school, there are some strategies you can use to help him overcome these issues:

- Try not to make too much of your child's shyness. If you frequently refer to him as being shy, this can exacerbate the problem making him feel shy, anxious and lacking in self-esteem.

- Sometimes a shy child is actually just cautious and wants to be certain of people and of situations before getting involved. This isn't always a bad thing and it may be helpful to describe your child as naturally cautious rather than shy.

- Shyness is only a problem if you feel it is holding your child back in some way, either socially or at school.

- One of the best ways to encourage your child to be more confident is to let him see that you are confident in social situations and to lead by example. Watching how you interact with others will help him understand how to do this successfully himself.

- Always make time to listen to what your child has to say. Allow him to have a voice, and don't dismiss any feelings of shyness or anxiety he expresses. Recognise his worries and try to suggest ways of dealing with them rather than implying that they are insignificant or unimportant.

- Many shy children feel more confident in the familiar surroundings of their own home, so try to invite your child's friends round to your house when you can. If you can invite a group round together, this may help him to feel more confident in social situations with a number of other children.

- Encourage your child to get involved – to go to parties and on outings, for example. Don't immediately suggest that he should avoid anything that he may find difficult, but try to help him to overcome his worries by focusing on the positive aspects of any events that you know he will enjoy.

- If your child is really worried about doing something, don't ever force him into situations that he's really not happy about. You may be able to find ways to ease him into social events; for example, ask another parent if it would be okay if you came along to their child's party and offer to help so that your child can feel more confident about attending the event. Other people will generally be sympathetic to your child's needs if you explain the situation.

- You will need to think carefully about maintaining a balance as it is important not to over-involve yourself in your child's life and not to do too many things for him – you want to encourage him to gain confidence in his own abilities.

- Try to find gradual ways to get him involved in things. If he's interested in an after-school activity such as a music class or a sports group but doesn't feel confident about joining, you could take him along to watch a few sessions before trying to get him to take part himself.

- Don't let your child see that you are worried about how he will cope with things. Of course you should always recognise any fears he expresses, but try not to fall into the trap of deciding that he is going to find something difficult in advance.

- Make sure you always praise him when he has done something that you know he has found difficult or challenging.

- Try not to worry too much as most shy children do find ways to deal with situations and many shy children grow into perfectly confident adults.

Sometimes shyness can go beyond a normal awkwardness in social situations and children can show tendencies to withdraw completely and to become very nervous and unhappy. If you feel your child's lack of confidence is something more than shyness, it is a good idea to talk to a teacher or to your GP about this.

Gifted and Talented Children

Not all children develop at the same pace, and those who are significantly ahead of others of their age may be identified as being gifted and talented. Children who are 'gifted' will be ahead of their peer group in one or more academic subjects, such as English and maths, and those who are 'talented' have skills in practical areas such as music, sport, art or drama.

Even at an early age, some children may show signs of being gifted; they may start to communicate at an earlier age than others and have an advanced vocabulary, they may learn quickly and ask lots of questions, they may start to read early and be good at puzzles, memory games and reasoning. If you think your child may be gifted, you should make sure that you mention his abilities when he first starts at school. Most gifted children do extremely well at school, but if their abilities are not recognised as they progress through the school and they are not sufficiently challenged, this can cause problems and they may lose motivation and underachieve. They may find it hard to fit in with others and can be sensitive and lacking in confidence and self-esteem.

Schools identify children who are gifted and talented in order to help them to achieve their full potential by making sure that they are sufficiently challenged at school. They may do this by providing different or additional work for them or even providing extra activities outside the normal school timetable. It is up to the school to decide which children are suitable for any extra opportunities and they will look at their work and take teachers' views into consideration as well as any test results. Generally the gifted and talented are considered to be the top 5–10 per cent of children in the school, so what constitutes gifted and talented at one school may not be the same as at another. Some schools will tell parents that their child has been identified as being gifted and talented, but other schools find that this can lead to problems and may offer children extra work or support in a more subtle way.

Gifted and talented children are sometimes identified in their first few months at school, but the extra help or support that they may receive can vary considerably. If your child is very far ahead of the others in his class and you are concerned that he isn't being stretched at all, it is a good idea to discuss this with his teacher. Most bright children will be fine in a normal class, but those who are way outside the normal range can get bored and lose impetus at school if they aren't given appropriate work. Gifted children can sometimes have a wide discrepancy between their intellectual development and their social and emotional development, which may make friendships and social interaction difficult for them. If your child is gifted, it will be helpful to seek help from a specialist organisation such as the National Association for Gifted Children (see Resources page 203) and to make contact with other parents of gifted children.

Special Educational Needs

Some children who struggle with communication, learning, their development or their behaviour may have special educational needs. They may find it hard to relate to others and to behave properly, have difficulties with speech or language, find it hard to understand or to think clearly, or have physical or sensory difficulties. There is a huge variety of issues that may come under the special needs umbrella: hearing or visual impairments, specific or general learning difficulties, behavioural problems, communication difficulties or medical conditions that may affect children's education. Depending on the severity of the difficulty, these problems may be apparent at a very early age and may be identified at this point by parents, a GP or a health visitor. In other cases, it may take a while for the special educational needs to be spotted. If you suspect that your child does have a specific difficulty, you should start by talking to his teacher who may refer you to the person in the school who has responsibility for dealing with children with special educational needs. This person is usually known as the SENCO, or Special Educational Needs Co-ordinator.

It is important to remember that all children develop in different ways and at different stages. Children who are slower to learn do not necessarily have any special educational needs.

Many children with special needs can continue to be taught within the mainstream schools system, but may need extra support or specific learning plans in place. They may have difficulties understanding at school, and may have problems with literacy and numeracy; they may have problems expressing themselves and find it hard to relate to others; or they may have behavioural difficulties or physical or sensory needs that require special help.

If the school feels your child has special educational needs, he should be given extra help and support. The school may start with an action plan to try to help your child in the classroom, which may involve offering extra support and help or teaching him in a slightly different way. This may be sufficient to help your child, but if it is felt that he needs more help, he may also be given an individual education plan to help monitor his development and to ensure that he is making sufficient progress. Children who clearly have specific learning problems should be formally assessed for a statement of special educational needs, which will explain what the child's needs are and what support should be offered.

Sometimes when children have more complex needs, or when they are not making progress, it may be necessary to get support from specialists outside the school who can offer additional expert help. In some cases if a child has needs that cannot be met in a mainstream school, it may be necessary to consider a special school that can offer the right kind of support. Getting the right kind of help for your child isn't always easy, and it is important that you are a part of any decisions made about your child's future. Children who have special needs should be regularly assessed to ensure that their needs continue to be met.

Autism

Autism is a form of developmental disability that can affect people in different ways and with different degrees of severity. People with autism are often described as having autistic spectrum disorders because, although they will have some common characteristics, each individual will be affected differently. For some, it may mean that they have quite serious learning problems and need considerable support, while others are more able to get on with their lives independently. Autism affects about one in every hundred people in the UK. It is still not entirely understood why some people are autistic, but it may be a combination of genetic and environmental factors. It is not anything parents can prevent or cure.

Autism affects the way that individuals relate to those around them and they often struggle to make sense of the world. While most of us know how to communicate with others and how to interpret their facial expressions and body language without even thinking about it, this can be very difficult for people who are autistic. Autism can also affect the senses of sight, sound, smell, taste and touch and the way that individuals react to these. The reactions that people with autism have and the way they are affected is often completely different; so some people with autism might hate bright lights and loud noises, they may hate being touched or may not like certain smells, while others may particularly like all these things.

People with autism are often very good at one thing, perhaps maths or music or art, and may be very focused on one activity. They may like repetitive things, so want to always eat the same food or to talk about one subject. They can find it hard to chat to other people and to join in with games or activities. They sometimes have problems with co-ordination and can find certain practical activities difficult.

One form of autism is Asperger syndrome. People who have Asperger syndrome are often very bright and don't usually have any difficulties with their language, but have problems with communication and interaction with other people.

Autism and Asperger syndrome are both life-long conditions for which there is no cure. There are three key areas where people will have problems:

- **Social skills:** People who are on the autistic spectrum usually have few social skills. They find it difficult to relate to other people because they don't always understand how to make small talk. This means that they may find it hard to make friends. They are not always aware of what is appropriate in conversation.

- **Communication skills:** Some people with autism find it hard to talk, and others who don't have any problems with language may find it difficult to understand any subtlety in conversation or to read other people's feelings or emotions. They may completely miss or misread the signals most of us pick up on without even thinking, such as facial expressions or gestures and body language. This can mean that they come across as being insensitive or rude.

● **Social imagination:** People with autism often find it hard to understand abstract ideas and may not be able to understand concepts outside normal day-to-day life. They may not be able to deal with anything that is not familiar to them, or to think about the future. This may mean that they have very little concept of danger, too.

There are some warning signs that may indicate that a child could have problems, and even from a very early age you may feel that something isn't quite right. The most common issues that you may spot are often to do with language and communication as a child may not seem to respond in the way that you would expect. Signs that could suggest autism may include:

1. Language skills may be delayed from an early age.

2. May have difficulty communicating.

3. Lack of facial expression and body language.

4. Difficulties making eye contact.

5. May not always respond and may sometimes not seem to hear you.

6. May seem to have problems with co-ordination.

7. May be very resistant to any change in daily routines.

8. May not seem interested in other children and may prefer to play alone.

9. May have difficulty joining in with any kind of imaginative play.

10. May seem to be in a world of his own.

11. May become obsessed with certain objects.

12. May seem to have regressed where communication and language skills are concerned.

It is sometimes very clear that a child has problems from an early age, but for those who are more able, it can take time for less obvious symptoms to be diagnosed. If you do have any concerns that your child could have an autism spectrum disorder, it is important to talk to your GP about your concerns right away and to have a proper assessment. Children are not usually diagnosed until the age of three, but doctors may use a checklist for younger children to see whether they appear to have problems which could suggest autism. It is important to get the right diagnosis so that your child can receive appropriate support.

Dyslexia

Dyslexia is a learning difficulty that can affect reading, writing, spelling and numeracy, as well as speech and vocabulary. It is often assumed that dyslexia cannot be identified until a child has begun to master reading and writing because it mainly affects these skills. In fact, it can sometimes be possible to identify dyslexic traits in a child at a relatively early age. There are some signs that may suggest a problem with dyslexia in younger children:

1. They may be slow to learn to speak.

2. They may find it difficult to dress themselves and to do up buttons.

3. They may find it hard to put their shoes on the right feet.

4. They may confuse, forget or jumble up words, sometimes using the wrong one by mistake.

5. They may find it hard to match rhyming words.

6. They may not remember nursery rhymes and can find it hard to clap in time.

7. They may seem clumsy, often tripping over things.

8. They may have co-ordination problems and find it hard to catch or throw a ball, or to skip.

9. They may find it hard to remember sequences, such as days of the week or numbers.

10. They may not seem to pay attention.

11. Although they may enjoy being read to, they may not show any interest in letters or words.

12. They may have some difficult days without any apparent reason for this.

Once children begin school and start to learn to read and write, dyslexic traits may become more apparent. A child may have difficulty with reading, finding it hard to decode words. They may also have problems with writing, using letters or figures the wrong way round. When trying to spell, they may get letters in the wrong order or leave some letters out altogether. They may find it hard to concentrate and can appear to be slower than other children when it comes to written work. They may not seem to understand what they've read. This can be frustrating for parents as dyslexic children are often very bright in other ways, but they can lack confidence due to the problems they are experiencing.

If you think that your child may be dyslexic, the first step is to talk to his class teacher and possibly the special educational needs co-ordinator at the school, too. An individual education plan may be recommended for your child to help ensure he is making appropriate progress. Some schools are very good at dealing with dyslexia and will be able to offer specific support and suggest ways that you may be able to help your child, but others are less experienced at helping children with dyslexia and may not be as forthcoming with help and advice. One problem many parents encounter is difficulties getting a formal assessment of their child's dyslexia as this can take some time unless you are willing or able to pay for it to be done privately. Sometimes children who are considered to be only mildly dyslexic will not receive much help or support. Only children who have quite significant problems will be given a statement of special educational needs, which sets out the help that they should be getting.

Dyspraxia

Dyspraxia affects the way the brain processes information and this in turn causes difficulty with movement as messages from the brain are not transmitted effectively. People with dyspraxia may have problems with their language, perception and thought processes.

It is thought that dyspraxia affects up to 10 per cent of the population, and it is far more common among boys than girls – they are four times more likely to be dyspraxic. Dyspraxia can sometimes be spotted at a very early age; babies may not ever crawl, going straight from bottom shuffling to walking, they may be irritable and may have feeding problems. By the time children reach pre-school age, there are often clear indicators that there may be a problem:

1. They may find it hard to sit still and may fidget a lot, tapping their feet or hands.

2. They are often clumsy, tripping over things.

3. They may have poor co-ordination and may have problems using scissors or pens, riding trikes or catching and throwing balls.

4. They may not seem to have a normal sense of what might be dangerous.

5. They are often very messy eaters, spilling things or using their fingers.

6. They may have very limited concentration.

7. They may have difficulty with language.

8. They may find it hard to get on with other children and may seem isolated.

9. They may not enjoy imaginative or creative play.

10. They may not seem to understand instructions.

11. They may be very excitable and prone to tantrums.

If you suspect that your child may be dyspraxic, you should talk to your GP or health visitor and your child's teacher. It is important to get a diagnosis so that your child can be offered appropriate help and support. Children with dyspraxia can be given focused help with their school work and with physical activities. Although dyspraxia cannot be 'cured', this kind of support can help children to overcome some of the symptoms and to minimise the problems they cause in daily life.

Dyscalculia

Dyscalculia is similar to dyslexia, but affects the ability to understand numbers rather than the ability to deal with words and letters. Children with dyscalculia do not have an intuitive understanding of numbers and find it really difficult to understand the most basic number facts or concepts. Dyscalculia is not as widely understood or recognised as dyslexia, but it is believed that it may be related to one specific area of the brain not functioning properly.

It is believed that up to 6 per cent of the population suffer with dyscalculia and they generally don't have any learning problems in other areas. Dyscalculia is sometimes linked with dyslexia, and about half of those who have dyslexia will also have problems with maths. This is sometimes due to difficulties with words making it hard for them to grasp concepts rather than a specific problem with numbers, and many dyslexics are good at maths – indeed, some have very advanced numeracy skills.

It is not usual to spot dyscalculia until children begin formal learning, but there may sometimes be early indicators that a child has problems understanding number concepts. They:

1. Are often slower to learn to count.

2. May find it very difficult to remember simple mathematical facts such as number bonds (a simple addition sum which has become so familiar that a child can recognise it and complete it almost instantly) or times tables.

3. May show a lack of understanding about numbers, so they may not be able tell whether one number is bigger than another.

4. May find it difficult to match a number to a quantity.

5. May continue to count objects individually when others can just see that there are three or four objects.

6. May find it hard to understand that a number written numerically is the same as a number written in words – so that ten is the same as 10.

7. Often find it hard to tell the time.

8. May confuse left and right.

9. Often lack confidence in their maths ability.

Having a child assessed for dyscalculia is far more difficult than getting an assessment for dyslexia because there are not the same kind of standardised established tests. Dyscalculia is not as widely recognised either, and so it can be hard to know how best to help a child who shows signs of dyscalculia. Children with dyscalculia tend to lack confidence when it comes to maths and one of the most important ways to try to help them is to build confidence by going back to basics. If you suspect your child has a specific problem with maths, talk to his class teacher.

Although dyscalculia affects relatively few children, maths anxiety is far more common and can lead to similar problems where children who are otherwise bright appear to struggle with numeracy. Maths anxiety is not always recognised, but confidence is key when it comes to achievement in numeracy. Researchers have found that people who experience maths anxiety have a fear response to sums in just the same way that the brain reacts in people who have other phobias, and that this reduces their problem-solving skills. If you suspect your child may be losing confidence in maths, giving him lots of extra maths to do at home in order to try to improve his numeracy skills can be counter-productive. Using some of the general tips to help develop these skills in a more subtle way (see page 112), such as getting your child to weigh things when you are cooking or playing games like dominos or Snakes and Ladders, will be more helpful. Some parents find that teaching a child simple relaxation techniques, such as using deep breathing when faced with sums that they think are going to be difficult, can make all the difference.

ADHD

Attention Deficit Hyperactivity Disorder, or ADHD, is a problem that affects up to 9 per cent of children. It is more commonly found in boys than in girls and treatment often includes medication. Many of the signs of ADHD may be found among other children and adults who don't have the disorder, but not with the same severity or frequency. Parents may first notice signs of ADHD at an early age and the condition is most commonly diagnosed when a child is between the ages of 3–7. These signs may include:

1. Being easily bored.

2. Restlessness.

3. Not listening when spoken to.

4. Daydreaming.

5. Often losing things.

6. Finding it hard to follow instructions.

7. Finding it difficult to process information.

8. Difficulty learning new things.

9. Fidgeting.

10. Finding it hard to sit still or be quiet.

11. Difficulty carrying out tasks quietly.

12. Impatience.

13. Being very impulsive.

There is no 'cure' for ADHD but many people successfully manage their symptoms. It is generally believed that the disorder is likely to be caused by a combination of genetic and environmental factors, for example, exposure to toxins such as cigarette smoke or alcohol during pregnancy. There have also been suggestions that there could be links between ADHD and diet or watching too much television.

If you think your child may have ADHD, your GP should be your first port of call. The GP may suggest some strategies to try to help or may refer you straight on to a specialist for proper diagnosis. ADHD is often treated with medication to help overcome the symptoms of the disorder, but therapy may also be recommended. Sometimes a change of diet or supplements may be suggested.

Speech Problems

It can be hard to gauge whether a child has a problem with speech and language as all children develop at different rates, and so parents may not be sure when being a little slow or behind with speech turns into a problem. If you are worried that your child doesn't seem to be speaking in the same way as others of the same age and you feel that he may have delayed development, you should talk to your GP or health visitor.

Speech and language problems can take a number of different forms. There may be a simple delay in development where a child just takes longer than others to learn to speak, or there may be more specific difficulties with articulation or with remembering words or sounds. Sometimes a child may develop a stammer or stutter. Children who have any form of language or speech problem may be referred to a speech therapist if this is felt to be appropriate so that they can be properly assessed and given the right kind of support.

Disability

If your child has a disability, you may need to think about what would be the best sort of school for him. Many children with disabilities are educated in mainstream schools, but some primary schools are better able to support children with disabilities than others.

You will want to be certain that the school buildings are accessible and safe for your child. In some schools there will be ramps, accessible toilets and even lifts, but this is not the case everywhere and it is important to think about your child's needs and what a school can offer. You may also want to find out whether there are other children with disabilities at the school, as it may be far easier for your child if he doesn't feel he stands out or is always different to the others.

General Tips and Advice

Whatever the nature of your child's problem, the most important thing that you can do as a parent is to make sure you give your support and understanding. Listen to your child and take what he has to say into account, talk to his teachers or to medical professionals who may be involved and make sure that you are all working towards the same goal of helping your child to achieve his full potential.

Schools today aim to be inclusive, encompassing a wide range of abilities and difficulties, and it is important for children to feel that they are a valued part of their school community whatever the nature of their difficulty. You not only want your child to achieve academically, but also to feel socially confident and to be happy and at ease throughout his school life.

Case History: Ruby – Dyslexia

We didn't notice anything unusual about Ruby's development until she started primary school. All the way through nursery she'd been bright and chatty, and she'd always had lots of friends. She'd loved being at nursery and there had never been any suggestion that anything might be wrong. She didn't have any interest in learning the alphabet or numbers when we tried to encourage her to have a go, but we weren't worried because she was still young and we thought she had plenty of time to get on with those things at primary school.

Once she started school, it didn't take long for Ruby to start lagging behind her friends. She couldn't seem to focus on things in the way that the others did and she wasn't making much progress with reading at all. It seemed odd because she'd always loved books and having stories read to her, but nothing seemed to sink in when it came to reading herself. We kept reassuring ourselves that it did just click for some children later than others.

Ruby was struggling with learning to write, too. At first, I thought maybe she was just doing things at a different pace, but it didn't seem to get any better as time went on. She got letters muddled up and when she attempted to write it was impossible to read what she'd written. Her maths wasn't much better, and she was lacking in confidence about anything to do with school. I remember once when it was her birthday and she had all the girls in her class over for her party and I was shocked when I looked at the cards; they'd all written them so beautifully and it was a wake-up call for me as it made me realise how far ahead her friends were compared with Ruby.

I spoke to her class teacher, but she wasn't helpful. She said that children progressed at different rates and I got the impression she thought I was a really pushy mother and that Ruby was a bit lazy. It was a friend of mine who first suggested that Ruby might be dyslexic. One of her children had dyslexia, and she said I should get Ruby tested.

When we started to think about it, there had been signs that Ruby might be dyslexic outside school, too. She was a bit of a dreamer and quite scatty; she was always forgetting things and getting muddled. To us, it was just Ruby but we realised that perhaps it was related to the difficulty she was having at school.

We went to see the special educational needs co-ordinator at the school, but she seemed to think that Ruby was too young to be assessed. She said that Ruby wasn't that far below average with her levels anyway, and that it wouldn't be the sort of problem which would merit a lot of intervention.

In the end we paid for Ruby to be assessed privately. She was losing confidence all the time, and we didn't feel the teachers at school were really helping her. We took Ruby to an educational psychologist, which was expensive, but it was worth it as the tests showed that Ruby was definitely dyslexic, and gave lots of suggestions as to how she should be helped at school.

We ended up moving her to a school where they have very good support for children with dyslexia, and a far more sympathetic attitude altogether. Talking to other parents, the levels of support do vary tremendously from one school to another. Ruby has come on in leaps and bounds since moving, and it has really helped her to know that there's a reason why she finds some things more difficult than other children.

6

The Path Ahead

Your child starting school may herald a change for your whole family, but all too soon it will become a part of your daily routine. You will find that his school life becomes a part of your lives, too, but the degree to which you become involved is up to you. Your child will become gradually more independent as he makes his way through school over the coming years, but there will inevitably be some challenges along the way.

Supporting Your Child at School

Parents spend a lot of time worrying about getting their child into the right school, but research shows that what makes most difference to children's achievement is not the school that they attend but rather the level of parental involvement in their education. There are lots of things that you can do to support your child's learning at school, and to make sure that he is able to achieve his full potential.

- Always ask your child about his day at school and what he has been doing. He may not always want to talk about it and you should respect this, but don't let that stop you showing an interest.

- If your child is given homework or reading to do at home, he is not yet old enough to remember this himself or to schedule time for it. Make sure you are aware of what he needs to do, and help him to find time for it.

- Get involved by listening to him read, making a quiet space for him to do any other homework and talking to him about what he has to do. Be ready to lend a hand if he needs assistance.

- Try to always attend any curriculum evenings or parents' evenings at school so that you know what your child will be covering during the year. If you can't attend a meeting, contact your child's teacher and ask whether it might be possible to find another time to run through the information quickly or whether there were any hand-outs you could have.

- Read regularly with your child and ensure he has a wide range of books available apart from his school reading books. A primary school child will still enjoy a bedtime story and time for this should be factored into his routine.

- Encourage your child's interests by seeking out books about the subjects that interest him, whatever they may be.

- Joining a local library can be really useful as it means your child has a ready supply of books to choose from.

- Keep up with the suggestions for helping build numeracy skills listed earlier in this book (see page 112), such as involving your child in weighing and measuring in cooking. This will help him see how important the skills he is learning are in his everyday life.

- Joining in with art or craft activities, playing music, and singing songs and nursery rhymes with your child will help him, too – it's not all about literacy and numeracy.

- Getting involved with the school and having good relationships with your child's teacher and other staff will help to give your child a positive feeling about his school.

- Finally, making sure your child arrives in good time and in the right uniform every day will boost his confidence and ensure that his day gets off to a good start.

Getting Involved

When your child starts school, it may be the first time that part of his life is separate from yours – and that you are not in control of what happens to him and how he deals with things. This can seem like an exciting step forwards, but it isn't always easy to deal with initially. If you are able to spend time at your child's school, whether that is by volunteering to help out in the classroom, by giving a hand with the Parents' Association fundraising or by attending events put on for parents, you may find that having more of an insight into what goes on will help you to feel more involved.

Helping Out in the Classroom

Many schools ask for parent volunteers to come in to listen to young children read on a one-to-one basis, or to help with particular projects in the classroom. If you are a stay-at-home parent or work part-time, this may be something you could consider. It will not only give you an insight into how your child's school works and what his days are like, but will also give much-valued help to the teaching staff. Schools may also ask for volunteers to accompany the class on trips or days out, which is another opportunity for you to get to know your child's classmates and teacher while also lending a helping hand.

School Events

Most schools arrange a variety of events during the year, some of which are likely to be fundraisers organised by the Parents' Association or Friends of the School. There may also be other events organised by the school itself, such as concerts, plays, information evenings or social events. What is on offer will vary from school to school, but going along to these will help you to feel part of the community – and your child will probably enjoy you visiting his school, too.

Parents' Evenings

You will usually have at least one parents' evening a year during your child's time at school, but these events are approached in different ways at different schools. There may be an evening or event at the start of term that all parents can attend where you will find out more about the curriculum for the year ahead and how you can support your child in his learning. There will probably be at least one opportunity to meet your child's teacher individually to discuss your child's progress. If there are any specific issues you are concerned about or wish to find out more about, this is a good time to raise them. If there are a few topics you want to discuss, it can be helpful to jot down a note to remind yourself.

School Reports

Your child will normally have an annual report at the end of each year, although some schools may give more regular reports each term. What you'll find in the report varies from school to school, but it should tell you whether your child is meeting the expected levels for his age – some schools use computer software to produce reports to show this, which can seem rather impersonal. You may be told what level your child is at, but not all schools choose to give this information to parents in reports. If you are concerned about anything in your child's report, take this up with his teacher.

The Parents' Association

Most schools will have some kind of Parents' Association and joining this can be a way of becoming more involved in the school and of helping to raise funds. There is often a committee of parents who run the association, but each will work in its own way. The advantages of being involved in the Parents' Association are that it can help you feel part of the school community, it will enable you to meet other parents, you will be raising funds for the school and it can also be fun. It can, however, be time-consuming and hard work, and some parents feel that they simply don't have the spare time to devote to this kind of activity.

Becoming a Governor

Joining the board of governors of your child's school, or of the school board in Scotland, is a more formal way of becoming involved in the running of the school and of having a real say in the management. Parent governors are elected if there are a number of parents who are interested in the role, but some schools struggle to find anyone willing to stand and a parent who is keen can be directly appointed. Governors are involved in monitoring the progress of the school, agreeing budgets, setting policies and accountability. The governors will also play a role in appointing the school's head teacher and sometimes other staff, too. A governing body consists of not just parents, but also representatives from the staff, the community and the local authority. As a governor you will be expected to attend formal meetings and you will also usually be involved in smaller working groups or sub-committees, which will focus on specific issues. This is a voluntary role, but you would be able to claim for any expenses.

Making Friends at the School Gates

If you are a busy parent, dropping off your child and rushing off to work or to care for other children, you may initially feel excluded from the chatter at the school gates. Being a new parent can be daunting, and if you are shy it may take you back to your own feelings about starting school. It can seem as if everyone else has a group of friends and you are the only parent who is always alone – but remember that others are probably feeling exactly the same way. New parents sometimes say that other parents are in cliques, but those who know one another already, perhaps through having older children at the school, may not be aware that they can appear unwelcoming. Smiling and saying hello to people will go a long way, and getting involved in school activities or offering to help with fundraising events will quickly help you to build some friendships.

There are sometimes barriers between different groups of mothers and one of the biggest divides can lie between those who work and those who are at home full-time with their children. Some parents seem to feel this more acutely than others, and it may depend to some degree on your own attitudes and those of other mothers around you – not all working mums and their stay-at-home counterparts are at loggerheads. I think it is a great shame that these divisions can develop as they are often built on misunderstandings and assumptions. It's perfectly possible to approach motherhood in any number of different ways but to still have the same aims of doing the best for your children and wanting to do all that you can to help them towards a happy future.

If you feel that you don't really fit in with the other mothers at the school gate, don't let your own feelings influence your child's social life; encouraging him to have friends round for tea after school or at weekends can help you to meet other parents. It does sometimes take a while to discover parents who are on the same wavelength, but once you do lasting friendships can be made at the school gates and being open and friendly to other parents will help you and your child to feel more settled.

Breakfast and After-School Clubs

The school day is far shorter than the average working day, usually ending sometime in the mid-afternoon, which makes things difficult for working parents. If you don't have a friend or family member who can look after your child for this short period of time, you would have to pay someone for childcare, which is why after-school clubs are popular with working parents. They are usually relatively inexpensive and provide care from the end of school until around 6pm for children whose parents are not able to pick them up at the end of the school day. After-school clubs are often held on the school premises, although sometimes one club cares for children from a number of local schools, and they offer a range of activities for the children. As many parents also need to be at work before the start of the school day, breakfast clubs can offer childcare before school and will usually provide breakfast, too.

If you are likely to want a place in a breakfast or after-school club, you should put your child's name down for this as soon as you can as there are sometimes long waiting lists. For a child just starting at school, attending a breakfast and/or after-school club can make for an extremely long day, and you should bear this in mind – your child will be very tired by the time he gets home.

Extra-curricular Activities

Many schools offer a wide range of clubs that children can attend at lunchtime or after school and these may include activities such as football, gymnastics, arts, crafts, drama and language clubs. Extra-curricular activities can be great fun, but sometimes parents are more enthusiastic about these than their children. Do talk to your child first and establish whether he'd like to join any classes before you decide to enrol him. School can be very tiring for children in the first year, and your child may find it too much to have to go along to French at lunchtime or football after school when he is in his first year, even if these are things he might otherwise enjoy. If he is keen to try lots of extra-curricular activities himself, it may be a good idea to limit him to choosing one or two initially and seeing how he goes before filling up his lunch breaks and time after school with too many clubs.

The same rule applies for any classes or clubs your child already attends, or that you would like him to attend, outside school. A weekend sports, music or art club may be something he really enjoys, but do think carefully about after-school activities, particularly during the first term. A full day at school is exhausting and your child may really need some quiet time to relax at the end of the day until he is more used to school.

Competitive Parents

It is perfectly natural to feel proud of your child and of his accomplishments, but sometimes parental desire for a child to succeed can go too far. Remember that each child is an individual with his own strengths and weaknesses, and at this stage what you should be aiming for is to foster a love of learning in your child, making him feel that education can be fun. It is far better for a child to progress more slowly but to genuinely enjoy what he is doing than for him to be constantly pushed to achieve more, which can result in a child who feels he is never able to do quite enough to make his parents happy.

You may find you come across other parents who are very competitive and constantly compare their child with others. Sometimes what seems to be competitive parenting can just be a mother or father who is genuinely excited by what their child has achieved, and who hasn't thought how this might appear to others whose children haven't scaled such heights. However, there are some parents who seem to need their child to be the best at everything and to tell everyone else about this; they may want their child to be one step ahead of others on the school reading scheme, to always have the best parts in the Christmas play or to be recognised as gifted and talented. When you are faced with very competitive parents, it can be difficult not to get drawn into making comparisons but it is best to try to avoid getting involved. Remember that those who need their child to be the best at everything will inevitably find at some point along the line that those expectations cannot be met, often leading to a miserable child and frustrated parents.

How to Manage the School Holidays

Whether you are a stay-at-home parent or have a full-time job, the school holidays can be a challenge. There are usually breaks of around a fortnight at Christmas and Easter, shorter half-term breaks and a longer holiday of at least six weeks during the summer. Parents who both work full-time may find that they have to employ a childminder or au pair to cover the longer school holidays, but there are some other options that may be possible depending on your work pattern and whether you have any degree of flexibility. Many schools run holiday clubs, and these can be very useful if you are a working parent as they offer a variety of activities. In many areas there will also be a range of privately run clubs offering week-long activities during the holidays, often focused on sport, drama or art. These are particularly useful if you have a child who is interested in the activity offered, but these clubs often only operate for part of the day or for normal school hours, which can leave you with gaps at either end if you are working. Some couples stagger their annual leave over the summer holidays in order to look after their children, and if you have flexible working, do shift work or can sometimes work from home it may be possible to arrange things so that you can cover childcare between you.

Others rely on grandparents or their extended family to help cover longer holidays, but this is only really a possibility if you have family nearby. If you are working part-time, you may be able to arrange childcare swaps with another parent which can work very well as your child will benefit, too.

If you are at home, you may still find it hard to fill the longer holidays and to keep your child occupied. Days out are great fun, but can quickly become expensive. It is worth planning ahead and arranging some playdates for your child, too.

What to Do If Your Child is Unwell

Children are prone to picking up coughs and colds when they first start school or nursery as they are exposed to viruses that they might not have encountered before. If your child is really unwell, for example with a fever or sickness, the decision not to send him to school will be straightforward as it will be apparent that he would not be able to get up and go to school. It can be more difficult to decide whether a child should go in when he is not entirely on form.

Your child should certainly stay at home:

1. If he has a fever or high temperature (a temperature over 37.5 is considered a fever, see www.nhs.uk).

2. If he has a rash as these can herald illnesses such as measles, which are infectious. Your GP will be able to give advice on whether your child should attend school once the rash has been checked out.

3. A child who has sickness and diarrhoea should not go to school until he is completely well.

4. Generally children who have coughs and colds, mild headaches or mild sore throats may be fine to go to school. However, you should follow your instincts here – if your child also has a temperature or other symptoms, or if you feel he won't be able to participate at school, then it is better for him to stay at home.

If you are going to keep your child at home, you should call the school as early as you can or email them to let them know that your child will not be attending. Your school will have let you know how they prefer to be contacted with this information when your child first joined.

Bugs and Parasites

There is very little you can do to prevent your child from ever coming into contact with some of the common parasites that can cause havoc among primary school parents, but it is important to know how to recognise them and how to deal with them. Head lice, threadworm and scabies can all affect children of this age, as can ringworm, an infectious skin condition.

Head lice

Most children will get head lice at some time during their time at school, and girls who tend to have longer hair are often more at risk. Head lice spread very quickly from one child to another and frequent hair washing doesn't deter them at all. They can't live for long away from a human head, so can't survive on towels or in bedding. There are some signs to look out for that can indicate that your child may have head lice:

1. You may notice that your child starts scratching his head excessively.

2. He may complain that his head feels tickly or itchy.

3. If you look through his hair, you may spot tiny white spots attached to individual shafts of hair, often behind the ears or at the nape of the neck. They may look like dandruff, but you can tell that they aren't as they don't come loose if you ruffle the hair. These are the eggs, or nits.

4. You won't usually be able to spot any lice in the hair as they are very small, usually less than 4mm in length.

You will find a variety of medicated treatments for head lice on sale at your local pharmacy and you can use a nit comb (which has extra-fine teeth) with conditioner to comb out the lice from your child's hair. If you are going to use a medicated treatment, you should discuss it with the pharmacist as some of these insecticides are not suitable for younger children or those with allergies. Whichever method you use, you should repeat the process to ensure that any newly hatched lice are removed as it takes them up to 10 days to emerge from their egg cases. You should treat the whole family as it is easy for head lice to travel from one person to another.

Parents are often embarrassed when their child has head lice, but you do need to inform your child's school. Other parents may not realise their children have head lice unless the school brings it to their attention and this can result in a cycle of children being re-infected. Once you tell staff at school, they can warn other parents and all the children can be treated at the same time.

Threadworm

They may sound horrible, but apparently nearly half of all children will have had threadworm by the time they reach the age of 10, and they can easily spread to the rest of the family if you are not careful. There are some common signs to look out for:

1. Itching around the bottom, especially at night.

2. Restlessness at night.

3. Weight loss.

4. Irritability.

5. Reduced appetite.

6. You may be able to spot what look like tiny white threads in your child's stools.

7. At night, you may be able to see small white threads around your child's anus.

Threadworm live in the human intestines and are spread through their eggs, which females come out to lay at night around the anus. This can be very itchy for the child, who may then end up with eggs under his fingernails. Threadworm eggs can survive on clothes and bedding for some time, so they are transmitted easily from one child to another.

If you think your child has threadworm, your pharmacist will be able to recommend medication and the whole family will need to be treated – if you are pregnant or have younger children you may need to see your GP. You will need to follow strict hygiene measures for around six weeks, making sure to wash hands and scrub nails as well as washing all bedding, soft toys and towels and vacuuming and damp dusting. This will help to prevent your child and the rest of the family being re-infected.

Ringworm

Despite the name, ringworm does not involve worms at all – it is, in fact, a skin infection caused by a fungus. It is very infectious and can spread quickly. You can recognise ringworm by the red rash on the skin, which is rounded with a darker red/pink circle around the outside. If it is not treated, it can become blistered and raised. Usually a simple anti-fungal cream from the pharmacist is all that is needed to treat ringworm, but if the ringworm is on the scalp, if it persists or if it is in a young child, it is usually advisable to see your GP.

Scabies

These are tiny mites that burrow under the skin and lay eggs. They can spread easily among groups of children. They are most often found in between the fingers. The main symptom is itching, but you may also see small bumps in between the fingers or in other warm areas, such as the inside of elbows or knees, under the arms or groin and on the inside of the wrist. If you think your child may have scabies, you should seek medical advice from your GP and follow strict hygiene measures. Your child should stay at home until he has been treated.

Moving Onwards

During the first year of school, the focus is still very much on play-based education as the children gradually adjust from nursery. When children move into the next stage they will be expected to spend more time listening and concentrating. The day will become more structured, and it can seem a big change for a small child. Initially they may find it hard to sit still for longer periods, and may miss the freedom they enjoyed when they first started school where they were more able to move about the classroom. Most children do gradually adapt to this, and will soon be used to the structured day, which becomes more familiar as they move through the school.

At the start of your child's time in the early school years, he is still developing and you will gradually see his aptitude and abilities grow. He may be a child who has an instinct for numbers and who finds he loves mental arithmetic, he may discover he has an ear for music or that he is a natural actor or comedian, he may adore sports or decide that he'd rather spend his time drawing. If you can encourage your child's natural strengths, while supporting him with the subjects he finds more challenging, he will flourish and enjoy the school years ahead. You may find yourself that the playground that seemed rather daunting at first is soon full of familiar faces and even some friends, and that your entire family can reap the benefits of becoming part of the wider school community.

Final Thoughts

I have seen many of the hundreds of children I've looked after over the years go through school and have enjoyed catching up with them as teenagers and even young adults. My experiences have made me realise quite how quickly this time passes, and just how precious each stage of a child's development can be.

In my opinion, the most important thing about these early years in school is establishing solid foundations so that your child can build on them for the future. I know how difficult it can be for parents who are worried about making the right choices when it comes to a school or nursery for their child, but it is parental involvement that will really make the difference to your child's progress, and your support at this time will be key to what happens in the years that lie ahead. That doesn't mean that you should be constantly pushing your child, or trying to ensure that he is always one step ahead of his peers, but rather encouraging him to try to do his best and to feel proud of the progress he has made.

Education has become so focused on meeting targets that it is easy to forget that academic achievement is just one of many things that matter in life. Of course, you want your child to do well, you want him to fulfil his full potential and to feel that he is in a stimulating and secure environment where he can thrive academically, but you also want to ensure that his own individuality is nurtured, that he learns to have confidence in himself whatever his academic abilities. Children should feel that the things that they can do matter just as much as those that they find more challenging, and this will help them to be self-assured and above all to be happy. A child who is happy at school and who doesn't feel constantly pressured to be something he isn't is far more likely to succeed.

Some children will excel academically, but not everyone can be top of the class at every subject. What I think matters most is that a child is given all the opportunities there are to ensure that he fulfils his potential, and your encouragement will help him to do this. Helping to make the early days in nursery and school a positive experience and offering your encouragement will help your child to feel enthusiastic about his first steps into education – this is one of the most important gifts that you can give him as it will provide strong foundations to build on for the rest of his school career.

Setting your child off on a path in which he knows that he is valued for his own unique qualities and helping him to realise that learning can be fun and enjoyable will mean that whatever choices you make for his education, he will be well prepared to go on towards the next stages of his life and to a successful future.

Recommended Books

Starting School

Going to Playschool by Sarah Garland (Frances Lincoln)

When an Elephant Comes to School by Jan Ormerod (Frances Lincoln)

I Am Too Absolutely Small for School (Charlie and Lola) by Lauren Child (Orchard Books)

Going to School (Usborne First Experiences): Illustrated by Stephen Cartwright (Usborne Books)

Overcoming Shyness

When You're Shy by Elizabeth Crary (Parenting Press)

Molly Mouse is Shy: A Story of Shyness by Lynne Gibbs and Melanie Mitchell (Windmill Books)

Useful Resources

The British Dyslexia Association
www.bdadyslexia.org.uk

Council for Disabled Children
www.councilfordisabledchildren.org.uk

Department for Education
www.education.gov.uk

Dyspraxia Foundation
www.dyspraxiafoundation.org.uk

I Can: Helps Children Communicate
www.ican.org.uk

National Association for Gifted Children
www.nagc.org

The National Autistic Society
www.autism.org.uk

Acknowledgements

I would like to express my gratitude to all the parents I have worked with over the years. Their feedback has been enormous help in writing my books. I would also like to thank my publisher Fiona MacIntyre for her constant encouragement and faith in my work, and my thanks to my editor Samantha Jackson, and to the rest of the team at Vermilion for all their hard work on the book.

A special thank you to my agent Emma Kirby for her continued dedication and support, and to Kate Brian for her unfailing commitment, effort and thoughtful contribution to the book. Thank you to my wonderful PA Alison Jermyn, and to the team at contentedbaby.com for their support while I was writing this book and their wonderful work on the website.

And, finally, I am ever grateful for the huge support I receive from the thousands of readers and followers of my books who take time to contact me – a heartfelt thank you to you all and much love to your contented babies.

Gina Ford

Index

The Contented Baby
with Toddler Book

Written in the same reassuring, accessible style as her bestselling *The Contented Little Baby Book*, *The Contented Baby with Toddler Book* is full of practical tips and brilliant solutions that will calm and support all busy parents. Gina's easy-to-follow and adaptable routines are designed to help you structure your day and meet all the needs of your new baby and toddler.

£10.99

ISBN 9780091929589

Order this title direct from www.randomhouse.co.uk

The Contented
Toddler Years

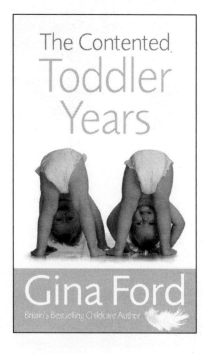

In *The Contented Toddler Years* Gina addresses the demands and needs of your growing toddler. She offers invaluable advice and insight into these crucial stages of a child's development, from walking and talking, to teething and potty training. Reassuring and down-to-earth, parents will find Gina's advice can help make the passage from contented baby to confident child a happy and stress-free experience for the whole family.

£10.99

ISBN 9780091912666

Order this title direct from www.randomhouse.co.uk